Blooming Crochet Creations

10 Designs for Kids and Adults With 15 Mix-and-Match Accents

Shauna-Lee Graham
of Bouquet Beanies

Fons&Porter

CINCINNATI, OHIO

Table of Contents

Introduction

I'm excited and honored to bring you this second Blooming Crochet book!

My first book featured hats and hair treasures, but this book includes ten fabulous designs for both kids and adults—five for each—as well as fifteen all new mix-and-match accents.

The fifteen new motifs in this book can be used on any of the projects from *Blooming Crochet Hats*, or vice versa—use any of the original motifs on these lovely accessories. There are innumerable ways to customize the look of your projects by simply switching the flowers and motifs to make each item unique.

I hope you enjoy these new designs. I had a blast creating them, and I'm excited to share them with all of you!

Enjoy, have fun and let your creativity shine!

—Shauna

Stitches & Techniques

Learn to Crochet

The stitches illustrated below will be used throughout the book. Use this guide if you aren't certain what to do or what a particular abbreviation means.

Slip Knot *(diag. 1)*

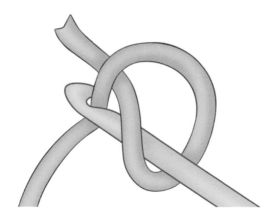

Form a loop, put the hook in the loop and draw another loop through.

Slip Knot *(diag. 2)*

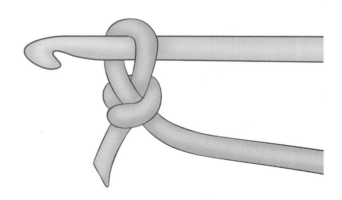

Slide the knot up the hook and tighten gently. Slip knot made.

Chain (ch)

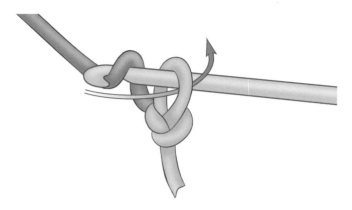

With the hook through the slip knot, yarn over (yo) and pull the yarn through the loop to make a new chain (ch).

Forming a Ring

Chain (ch) as many stitches (sts) as indicated, insert the hook in the 1st ch, yarn over (yo) and pull through the 1st ch and the ch on the hook.

Single Crochet (sc) *(diag. 1)*

Insert the hook into the 2nd chain (ch) from the hook, yarn over (yo) and draw the yarn through the work only.

Single Crochet (sc) *(diag. 2)*

Yo again and draw through both of the loops on the hook. Single crochet (sc) made.

Half Double Crochet (hdc)

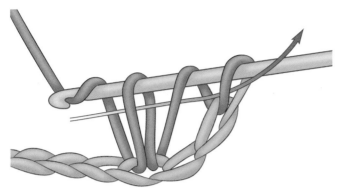

Yarn over (yo), insert the hook into the 3rd chain (ch) from the hook, yo and draw through the work only; yo and draw through all 3 loops on the hook. Half double crochet (hdc) made.

Double Crochet (dc) *(diag. 1)*

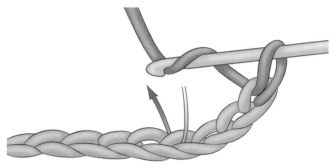

Yarn over (yo) and insert the hook into the 4th chain (ch) from the hook.

Double Crochet (dc) *(diag. 2)*

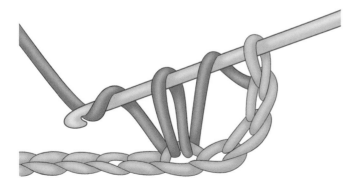

Yo, draw through the work only, yo and draw through the 1st 2 loops on the hook.

Double Crochet (dc) *(diag. 3)*

Yo and draw through the remaining 2 loops on the hook. Double crochet (dc) made.

Treble Crochet (tr) *(diag. 1)*

Yarn over (yo) twice, insert the hook into the 5th chain (ch) from the hook and draw up a loop.

Treble Crochet (tr) *(diag. 2)*

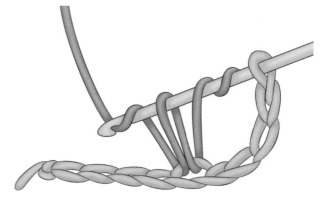

Yo and draw through 2 loops on the hook.

Treble Crochet (tr) *(diag. 3)*

Yo and draw through the next 2 loops on the hook.

Treble Crochet (tr) *(diag. 4)*

Yo and draw through the last 2 loops on the hook. Treble crochet (tr) made.

Slip Stitch (sl st)

Insert the hook into the 2nd chain (ch) from the hook. Yarn over (yo) and draw the yarn through both the work and the loop on the hook at the same time. Slip stitch (sl st) made.

Front Loop (flp) / Back Loop (blp)

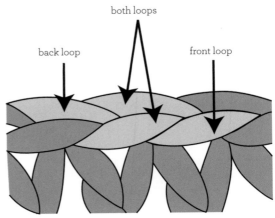

Work in the front strand or front loop (flp) or back strand or back loop (blp) as directed in the pattern.

Front Post Double Crochet (fpdc)

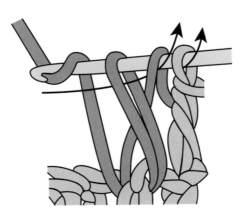

Yarn over (yo), insert the hook from the front to the back around post of the previous row, draw up a loop, yo, draw through 2 loops on the hook, yo and draw through the last 2 loops on the hook. Front post double crochet (fpdc) made.

Back Post Double Crochet (bpdc)

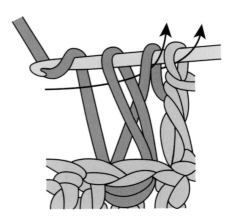

Yarn over (yo), insert the hook from the back to the front around the post of the previous row, draw up a loop, yo, draw through 2 loops on the hook, yo and draw through the last 2 loops on the hook. Back post double crochet (bpdc) made.

Changing Colors in Double Crochet (dc) *(diag. 1)*

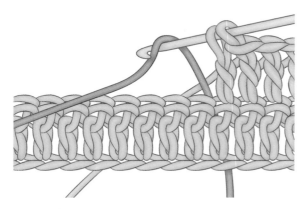

Proceed with a double crochet (dc) until 2 loops remain on the hook, then draw the new yarn through.

Changing Colors in Double Crochet (dc) *(diag. 2)*

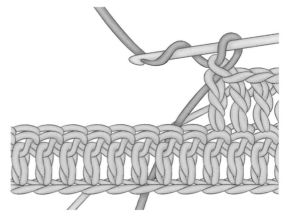

Yarn over (yo).

Changing Colors in Double Crochet (dc) *(diag. 3)*

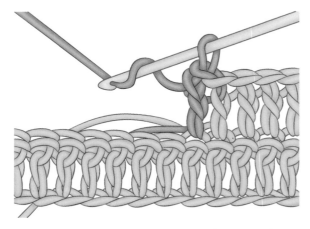

Proceed with a dc in the new color. Cut the yarn color you are not using and secure the ends behind the work.

3 Double Crochet Cluster Stitch (3dc-cl)

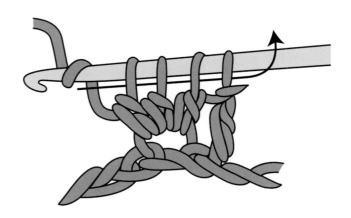

(Yarn over [yo], insert the hook in the stitch [st] indicated, draw up a loop, yo, pull the yarn through 2 loops on the hook) 3 times, yo, draw through all 4 loops on the hook. 3 double crochet cluster (3dc-cl) made.

Half Double Crochet Decrease (hdc dec) *(diag. 1)*

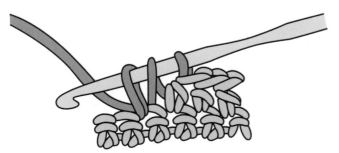

Yarn over (yo), insert the hook in the stitch (st), yo and draw up a loop.

Half Double Crochet Decrease (hdc dec) *(diag. 2)*

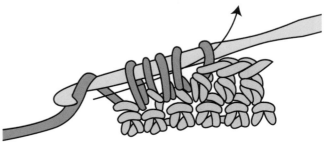

Yo, insert the hook in the next st, yo and draw up another loop.

Half Double Crochet Decrease (hdc dec) *(diag. 3)*

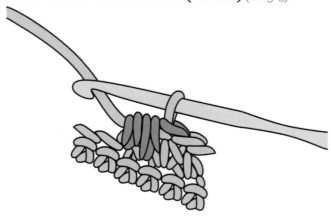

Yo and draw through the 5 loops on the hook. Half double crochet decrease (hdc dec) made.

Double Crochet Decrease (dc dec) *(diag. 1)*

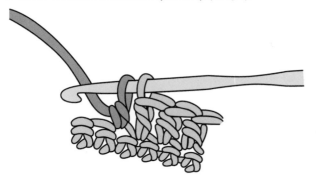

Yarn over (yo), insert the hook in the stitch (st), yo, draw up a loop, yo and draw through 2 loops.

Double Crochet Decrease (dc dec) *(diag. 2)*

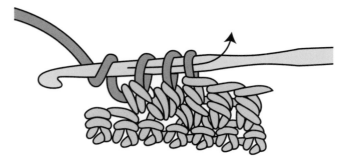

Yo, insert the hook in the next st, yo, draw up a loop, yo and draw through 2 loops.

Double Crochet Decrease (dc dec) *(diag. 3)*

Yo and draw through the 3 loops on the hook. Double crochet decrease (dc dec) made.

Picot Stitch (diag. 1)

Chain (ch) 3, insert the hook through the front loop (flp) of the base stitch (st) and the left vertical bar of the base st.

Picot Stitch (diag 2)

Yarn over (yo) and draw through all the loops on the hook. Picot st made.

Popcorn Stitch (pc)

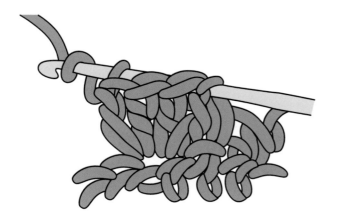

Work 4 double crochet (dc) in the same stitch (st), then take the loop off the hook and insert the hook into the 1st dc st; place the loop you took off the hook onto the hook and draw that loop through the loop (1st dc st) on the hook. Popcorn (pc) made.

Treble Crochet Bobble Stitch (trbs)

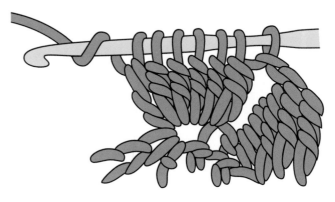

Working in the same stitch (st), (yarn over [yo] twice, insert the hook in the st, draw up a loop, yo, draw through 2 loops on the hook, yo, draw through 2 loops on the hook) 6 times, yo, draw through all 7 loops on the hook. Treble crochet bobble stitch (trbs) made.

Slip Stitch Border (*diag. 1*)

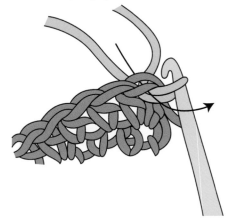

Using the trim color (TC) of your choice, insert the hook through any stitch (st) on the last round of the work. Draw the yarn up through the st.

Slip Stitch Border (*diag. 2*)

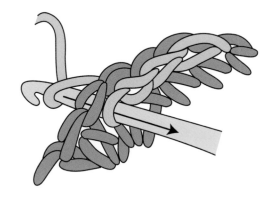

Insert the hook into the next st and slip stitch (sl st) around the outside of the entire shape to the last st.

Slip Stitch Border (*diag. 3*)

After slip stitching in the last st, drop the loop off your hook and place the hook under the work. Insert the hook from the bottom, up into the center of the 1st sl st made. With your fingers, place the loop over the hook and draw it down through the center of the 1st sl st. Cut the yarn and pull the end through the loop. Pull tight, tie both ends together and weave in the ends.

About Buttons

We all know that young children like to put things in their mouths. They must be watched at all times while wearing items with buttons due to choking hazards. If you're concerned that your child might try to eat the buttons on the projects in this book, try making the crochet button alternative below.

Crochet Button Alternative

Using a small amount of sport weight yarn and leaving a 7" (17.8cm) yarn tail, ch 2.

Rnd 1: Work 8 hdc in 2nd ch from hook; join with sl st in beg hdc (8 hdc).

Rnd 2: Ch 1, (insert hook in 1st hdc, draw up loop, insert hook in next hdc, draw up loop, yo, draw through all 3 loops on hook) 4 times, join with a sl st to beg hdc (4 dec made).

Fasten off.

Insert the 7" (17.8cm) yarn tail into the bottom of the button to create a filling. Using a tapestry needle, thread the other end of the yarn, gather the opening of the button, draw tight and tie.

Glossary of Abbreviations

3dc-cl	3 double crochet cluster
beg	beginning
blp(s)	back loops only
bphdc	back post half double crochet
bptr	back post treble crochet
ch(s)	chain(s)
dc	double crochet
dc dec	double crochet decrease
dec	decrease
flp(s)	front loops only
hdc	half double crochet
hdc dec	half double crochet decrease
pc	popcorn stitch
prev	previous
rep	repeat
rnd(s)	round(s)
RS	right side
sc	single crochet
sk	skip
sl st	slip stitch
sp(s)	space(s)
st(s)	stitch(s)
tr	treble crochet
trbs	treble crochet bobble stitch
WS	wrong side
yo	yarn over
*	repeat instructions following the asterisk as directed
( )	work instructions within parentheses as many times as directed

About Skill Levels

At the beginning of each project, you'll notice a flower symbol that denotes the skill level necessary to successfully complete the project. Here's a guide for the difficulty of those levels.

 Beginner. These projects are excellent for first-time crocheters. They use basic stitches and have minimal shaping.

 **Easy/Intermediate**. These projects use basic stitches, repetitive stitch patterns, simple color changes and simple shaping and finishing.

Chapter 1
Fun for Kids

I can't think of a better way to enjoy a beautiful day than by having a family picnic under the warm, summer sun. I can picture it now. The Popping Chevron Blanket is spread out on the thick, green grass with all the delicious goodies we made gathered in the middle. The baby is dressed in his little Bloomers & Britches with the rear flap sewn onto the bottom (which will look adorable in those keepsake photos!). The kids' Shoulder Packs are stuffed with all those little knickknacks to pass the day away, including their favorite Tic-Tac-Toe Travel Game, which they love to play using the hand-picked game pieces their grandma made them for their birthday. And don't forget about the little girl's Bassinet Purse. She never leaves home without it, because with just a simple fold, this little bag turns into a magical world for a girl and her most treasured doll.

Adorable Bassinet Purse

This is a new take on an old classic. Just fold down the sides of this purse, and it magically turns into a bassinet with a canopy. When it's in purse mode, it holds a doll, a blanket and a pillow. It also has room for those extra little knickknacks. Make one in your child's favorite colors so she can take her dolls with her anywhere. These would also be great to give out as loot bags at a birthday party.

MATERIALS

Worsted weight yarn **(4)** in the color of your choice

Color 1: 90 yds (83m)

Color 2: 140 yds (128m)

Size I (5.5mm) crochet hook

⅞"–1" (2.2cm–2.5cm) button

Polyester stuffing

Scissors

Tapestry needle

Finished Project Sizes

Purse: 3" wide × 9" long × 7" high (7.6cm × 22.9cm × 17.8cm)

Blanket: 6" × 4¼" (15.2cm × 10.8cm)

Pillow: 3¾" × 3" (9.5cm × 7.6cm)

Gauge

No gauge required.

Glossary of Abbreviations

beg	beginning
blp(s)	back loop(s)
bphdc	back post half double crochet
ch(s)	chain(s)
dc	double crochet
dc dec	double crochet decrease
flp(s)	front loop(s)
hdc	half double crochet
hdc dec	half double crochet decrease
prev	previous
rep	repeat
rnd(s)	round(s)
sc	single crochet
sk	skip
sl st	slip stitch
st(s)	stitch(es)
yo	yarn over
*	repeat instructions following the asterisk as directed
( )	work instructions within parentheses as many times as directed
C1	color 1
C2	color 2

See **Stitches & Techniques** for illustrated instructions for the double crochet decrease (dc dec) and half double crochet decrease (hdc dec).

Bassinet Purse

With C1, ch 21.

Rnd 1: Work 2 hdc in 3rd ch from hook, hdc in next 17 ch, 3 hdc in last ch. Working around the other side of the ch, work hdc in next 17 sts; join with sl st in 2nd ch of beg ch-2 (40 hdc).

Rnd 2: Ch 2, hdc in same st as joining, 2 hdc in next 4 sts, hdc in next 14 sts, 2 hdc in next 6 sts, hdc in next 14 sts, 2 hdc in last st; join with sl st in 2nd ch of beg ch-2 (52 hdc).

Rnd 3: Ch 2, 2 hdc in next 8 sts, hdc in next 18 sts, 2 hdc in next 8 sts, hdc in last 17 sts; join with sl st in 2nd ch of beg ch-2 (68 hdc).

Rnd 4: Ch 2, bphdc in next st and in each st around; join with sl st in 2nd ch of beg ch-2 (68 hdc).

Rnd 5: Ch 2, hdc in same st as joining and in each st around; join with sl st in 2nd ch of beg ch-2 (69 hdc).

Rnd 6: Ch 1, (sc, 2 dc) in same st as joining (shell made), * sk next 2 sts, (sc, 2 dc) in next st, rep from * around to last 2 sts, sk last 2 sts; join with sl st in beg sc (23 shells).

Rnd 7: Ch 2, hdc in next st and in each st around; join with sl st in 2nd ch of beg ch-2 (69 hdc).

Rnd 8: Ch 1, (sc, 2 dc) in same st as joining, sk next 2 sts, * (sc, 2 dc) in next st, sk next 2 sts, rep from * around; join with sl st in beg sc (23 shells).

Rnd 9: Ch 2, hdc in next st and in each st around; join with sl st in 2nd ch of beg ch-2 (69 hdc).

Rnd 10: Ch 1, (sc, 2 dc) in same st as joining, sk next 2 sts, * (sc, 2 dc) in next st, sk next 2 sts, rep from * around; join C2 with sl st in beg sc (23 shells).

Note: *Do not weave in ends for the joining of the 2 colors. This will be the guide stitch to make the canopy.*

Rnd 11: Ch 2, working in flps only, hdc in next st and in each st around; join with sl st in 2nd ch of beg ch-2 (69 hdc).

Rnds 12–15: Rep Rnds 8 and 9.

Rnd 16: Ch 1, sl st in next 7 sts, hdc in next 20 sts, sl st in next 14 sts, hdc in next 20 sts, sl st in last 7 sts; join with sl st in beg ch-1 (28 sl sts, 40 hdc).

Rnd 17: Do not ch, sl st in next 7 sl sts, hdc in next 20 hdc, ch 14, sk next 14 sl sts, hdc in next 20 hdc, ch 14, sk next 14 sl sts; join with sl st in next hdc (28 chs, 40 hdc).

Rnd 18: Ch 2, hdc in next 19 hdc, hdc in next 14 chs, hdc in next 20 hdc, hdc in next 14 chs; join with sl st in 2nd ch of beg ch-2 (68 hdc).

Rnds 19–20: Ch 1, sc in same st as joining and in each st around; join with sl st in beg sc (68 sc).

Rnd 21: Ch 1, sl st in same st as joining and in each st around; join with sl st in beg ch-1 (68 sl sts).

Fasten off.

Want to make just the purse? Simply work through both loops of Rnd 11 instead of through the front loops only, then continue with Rows 12–21 to complete the purse.

Bassinet Canopy

Fold the top half of the purse down to the color change at Rnd 10. Make sure the joining ends of C1 & C2 from Rnd 11 are toward you.

Insert hook in the blp of the 2nd st to the right of the joining end st and join C1.

Row 1: Ch 1, working in blps, sc in same st as joining and in next 27 sts (28 sc).

Row 2: Ch 2, turn, hdc in next 8 sts, dc in next 10 sts, hdc in last 9 sts (28 sts).

Row 3: Ch 1, turn, hdc dec, hdc in next 2 sts, dc dec, dc in next 2 sts, dc dec, dc in next 3 sts, dc dec, dc in next 2 sts, dc dec, dc in next 2 sts, dc dec, hdc in next 2 sts, hdc dec (20 sts).

Row 4: Ch 1, turn, hdc dec, hdc in next 2 sts, 2 dc dec, dc in next 4 sts, 2 dc dec, hdc in next 2 sts, hdc dec (14 sts).

Row 5: Ch 1, turn, sc in next st, hdc in next 2 sts, dc in next 8 sts, hdc in next 2 sts, sc in last st (14 sts).

Rnd 6: Do not fasten off and do not turn. Work 4 sl sts down the side of the canopy, then sc in same blp st of ending st of Row 1; working around the bassinet, sc in next 40 blps, join with sl st in beg sc of Row 1, then working up the canopy, work 20 hdc evenly across to the other side of canopy, join with sl st in next st.

Fasten off.

Bassinet Slip Stitch Trim

1. With C2, insert hook in next st.

2. Draw the yarn up through the st.

3. Insert hook into next st and sl st, proceed to sl st around the entire bassinet to the last st.

4. When you get to the last st, drop the loop off your hook; insert hook from bottom up into the center of the 1st sl st made. Pick up the loop with your fingers, place it over the hook and draw it down through the center of the 1st sl st.

5. Cut the yarn and pull the end through the loop. Pull tight and tie both ends together.

Weave in ends.

Cut a piece of yarn and tie a bow on the canopy.

Pillow

With C2, ch 11.

Row 1: Sc in 2nd ch from hook and each ch across (10 sc).

Rows 2–8: Ch 1, turn; sc in 1st st and in each st across (10 sc).

Row 9: Ch 1, turn; working in flps, sc in 1st flp and in each flp across (10 sc).

Rows 10–16: Rep Rows 2–8.

Do not fasten off.

Fold pillow in half to make 2 sides to the pillow, allowing the blps of Row 9 to face out. These blps will be used as one of the seams that you will sc around to crochet the pillow together.

Working through both loops on both sides of pillow:

Note: *You will be working the pillow slip stitch trim through the same loops worked through in Rnd 1.*

Rnd 1: Ch 1, do not turn, insert hook through the ending sc post of the sc you just made and sc, work 6 sc evenly down side, sc in next 10 blps across, work 7 sc evenly down side. Stuff the pillow through the open side using polyester stuffing or leftover yarn, then sc in the next st and in each st across; join with sl st in beg sc.

Fasten off. Hide ends by pulling them into the middle of the pillow with your crochet hook.

Pillow Slip Stitch Trim

1. With C1, insert hook into any st from Rnd 1 (see note in prev section).

2. Draw the yarn up through the st.

3. Insert hook into next st and sl st; proceed to sl st around the entire pillow to the last st.

4. When you get to the last st, drop the loop off your hook. Insert hook from the bottom up into the center of the 1st sl st made. Pick up the loop with your fingers, place it over the hook and draw it down through the center of the 1st sl st.

5. Cut the yarn and pull the end through the loop. Pull tight, tie both ends together and hide ends by pulling them into the middle of the pillow with your crochet hook.

Blanket

With C2, ch 13.

Row 1: Sc in 2nd ch from hook and in each ch across (12 sc).

Rows 2–20: Ch 1, turn; sc in 1st st and in each st across (12 sc).

Do not fasten off.

 Illustrated instructions for the slip stitch trim can be found in **Stitches & Techniques**.

Note: *You will be working the blanket slip stitch trim through the same loops worked through in Rnd 1.*

Rnd 1: Ch 1, do not turn, insert hook through the ending sc post of the sc you just made and sc, work 19 sc evenly down side, work 2 sc in corner st, sc in next 10 sts, 2 sc in corner st, work 20 sc evenly across side, 2 sc in corner st, sc in next 10 sts, then 2 sc in last st; join with sl st in beg sc.

Fasten off. Weave in ends.

Blanket Slip Stitch Trim

1. With C1, insert hook into any st from Rnd 1 (see note under *Blanket*).

2. Draw the yarn up through the st.

3. Insert hook into next st and sl st, proceed to sl st around the entire blanket to the last st.

4. When you get to the last st, drop the loop off your hook; insert hook from bottom up into the center of the 1st sl st made. Take the loop with your fingers, place it over the hook and draw it down through the center of the 1st sl st.

5. Cut the yarn and pull the end through the loop. Pull tight, tie both ends together, then weave in ends.

Finishing Touches

Sew a button onto the upper corner of the purse and attach your favorite motif from Chapter 3.

Bloomers & Britches

Looking for the perfect photo prop or an everyday wear item for your little one? These BLOOMERS & BRITCHES are simply adorable! There are many ways to customize these bottoms. Choose from the bloomers, which go to the knees, or the britches, which go to the ankles. Change the waistband color and choose either a straight leg with a cuff or a flared leg. There are also options for a knee patch and a rear flap.

MATERIALS

Main color: Sport weight yarn in the color of your choice

Bloomers:

  0–3 mos. (137–175 yds/126–160m)

  3–6 mos. (167–220 yds/153–202m)

  6–12 mos. (195–265 yds/179–243m)

Britches:

  0–3 mos. (185–210 yds/170–192m)

  3–6 mos. (215–255 yds/197–234m)

  6–12 mos. (240–300 yds/220–275m)

Trim color: Sport weight yarn 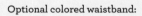 in the color of your choice

Optional colored waistband:

  0–3 mos. (30 yds/28m)

  3–6 mos. (40 yds/37m)

  6–12 mos. (45 yds/42m)

Size I (5.5mm) crochet hook

⅞"–1" (2.2cm–2.5cm) buttons (1 per motif and 2 if making the rear flap)

Tapestry needle

Scissors

Finished Project Sizes

To fit approx. 0–3 months:
Waistband circumference = 16" (40.6cm); waistband to crotch = 6" (15.2cm); waist to knee = 8½" (21.6cm); waistband to ankle = 12" (30.5cm)

To fit approx. 3–6 months:
Waistband circumference = 18" (45.7cm); waistband to crotch = 8" (20.3cm); waist to knee = 10½" (26.7cm); waistband to ankle = 14" (35.6cm)

To fit approx. 6–12 months:
Waistband circumference = 20" (50.8cm); waistband to crotch = 8" (20.3cm); waist to knee = 11" (27.9cm); waistband to ankle = 15" (38.1cm)

Gauge

15 st = 4" (10.2cm)

7 rows dc = 4" (10.2cm)

Glossary of Abbreviations

beg	beginning
blp(s)	back loop(s)
ch(s)	chain(s)
dc	double crochet
hdc	half double crochet
rem	remaining
rep	repeat
rnd(s)	round(s)
sc	single crochet
sl st	slip stitch
st(s)	stitch(es)
tr	treble crochet
yo	yarn over
*	repeat instructions following the asterisk as directed
( )	work instructions within parentheses as many times as directed
MC	main color
TC	trim color

Bloomers & Britches (0–3 months)

Waistband

With MC, ch 54, being careful not to twist the ch; join with sl st in beg ch.

Rnd 1: Ch 2 (counts as hdc), hdc in next ch and in each ch around; join with sl st in 2nd ch of beg ch-2 (54 hdc).

Rnd 2: Ch 3 (counts as dc), dc in next st and in each st around; join with sl st in 3rd ch of beg ch-3 (54 dc).

Rnd 3: Ch 2, hdc in next ch and in each ch around; join with sl st in 2nd ch of beg ch-2 (54 hdc).

Rnds 4–12: Ch 3, dc in next st and in each st around; join with sl st in 3rd ch of beg ch-3 (54 dc).

Do not fasten off. Continue with *Leg Hole 1*.

Add a Colored Waistband

Want to add a splash of color to your BLOOMERS & BRITCHES? Replace the main color yarn for the waistband with a complementary trim color, then join the main color on the last stitch of Round 3. See **Stitches & Techniques** for instructions on changing colors.

Leg Hole 1

Rnd 1 (splitting of legs): Ch 3, dc in next 25 sts, (yo, insert hook in next dc and directly through dc to the left of beg ch-3 and proceed to finish dc), leaving rem 26 dc unworked; join with sl st in 3rd ch of beg ch-3 (27 dc).

Rnds 2–3: Ch 3, dc in next st and in each st around; join with sl st in 3rd ch of beg ch-3 (27 dc).

Decide if you would like straight- or flared-leg bloomers or britches and proceed with the correct option below, starting with Rnd 4.

For Straight-Leg Bloomers

Rnd 4: Ch 3, dc in next st and in each st around; join TC with sl st in 3rd ch of beg ch-3 (27 dc).

Rnd 5: Ch 2, turn, working in blps only, hdc in next st and in each st around; join with sl st in 2nd ch of beg ch-2 (27 hdc).

Rnd 6: Ch 3, dc in next st and in each st around; join with sl st in 3rd ch of beg ch-3 (27 dc).

Rnd 7: Ch 2, hdc in next st and in each st around; join with sl st in 2nd ch of beg ch-2 (27 hdc).

Fasten off. Weave in ends. Fold pant cuff up.

For Flared-Leg Bloomers

Rnd 4: Ch 3, dc in next st and in each st around; join with sl st in 2nd ch of beg ch-2 (27 hdc).

Rnd 5: Ch 4, work 4 tr in same st as joining, * 5 tr in next st, rep from * around; join with sl st in 4th ch of beg ch-4 (135 tr).

Fasten off. Weave in ends.

For Straight-Leg Britches

Rnds 4–8: Ch 3, dc in next st and in each st around; join with sl st in 3rd ch of beg ch-3 (27 dc).

Rnd 9: Ch 3, dc in next st and in each st around; join TC with sl st in 3rd ch of beg ch-3 (27 dc).

Rnd 10: Ch 2, turn, working in blps only, hdc in next st and in each st around; join with sl st in 2nd ch of beg ch-2 (27 hdc).

Rnd 11: Ch 3, dc in next st and in each st around; join with sl st in 3rd ch of beg ch-3 (27 dc).

Rnd 12: Ch 2, hdc in next st and in each st around; join with sl st in 2nd ch of beg ch-2 (27 hdc).

Fasten off. Weave in ends. Fold pant cuff up.

For Flared-Leg Britches

Rnds 4–5: Ch 3, dc in next st and in each st around; join with sl st in 3rd ch of beg ch-3 (27 dc).

Rnd 6: Ch 3, dc in same st as joining, * dc in next dc, 2 dc in next dc, rep from * around; join with sl st in 3rd ch of beg ch-3 (41 dc).

Rnds 7–8: Ch 3, dc in next st and in each st around; join with sl st in 3rd ch of beg ch-3 (41 dc).

Rnd 9: Ch 4, work 4 tr in same st as joining, * 5 tr in next st, rep from * around; join with sl st in 4th ch of beg ch-4 (205 tr).

Fasten off. Weave in ends.

Leg Hole 2

With the top of the bloomers or britches facing you and the completed leg to the right, insert the hook directly through both dc (upper and lower) to the left of the completed leg (counts as one st); join MC.

Rnd 1: Ch 3, dc in same st as joining and in each st around to last st, 2 dc in last st, join with sl st in 3rd ch of beg ch-3 (27 dc).

Rnds 2–3: Ch 3, dc in next st and in each st around, join with sl st in 3rd ch of beg ch-3 (27 dc).

For Straight-Leg Bloomers

Work Rnds 4–7 the same as *Leg Hole 1 for Straight-Leg Bloomers*. Fasten off. Weave in ends. Fold pant cuff up.

For Flared-Leg Bloomers

Work Rnds 4–5 the same as *Leg Hole 1 for Flared-Leg Bloomers*. Fasten off. Weave in ends.

For Straight-Leg Britches

Work Rnds 4–12 the same as *Leg Hole 1 for Straight-Leg Britches*. Fasten off. Weave in ends. Fold pant cuff up.

For Flared-Leg Britches

Work Rnds 4–9 the same as *Leg Hole 1 for Flared-Leg Britches*. Fasten off. Weave in ends.

Add a Colored Waistband

Want to add a splash of color to your BLOOMERS & BRITCHES? Replace the main color yarn for the waistband with a complementary trim color, then join the main color on the last stitch of Round 3. See **Stitches & Techniques** for instructions on changing colors.

Bloomers & Britches (3–6 months)

Waistband

With MC, ch 60, being careful not to twist the ch; join with sl st in beg ch.

Rnd 1: Ch 2 (counts as hdc), hdc in next ch and in each ch around; join with sl st in 2nd ch of beg ch-2 (60 hdc).

Rnd 2: Ch 3 (counts as dc), dc in next st and in each st around; join with sl st in 3rd ch of beg ch-3 (60 dc).

Rnd 3: Ch 2, hdc in next ch and in each ch around; join with sl st in 2nd ch of beg ch-2 (60 hdc).

Rnds 4–13: Ch 3, dc in next st and in each st around; join with sl st in 3rd ch of beg ch-3 (60 dc).

Do not fasten off. Continue with *Leg Hole 1*.

Leg Hole 1

Rnd 1 (splitting of legs): Ch 3, dc in next 28 sts, (yo, insert hook in next dc and directly through dc to the left of beg ch-3 and proceed to finish dc), leaving rem 29 dc unworked; join with sl st in 3rd ch of beg ch-3 (30 dc).

Rnds 2–6: Ch 3, dc in next st and in each st around; join with sl st in 3rd ch of beg ch-3 (30 dc).

Decide if you would like straight- or flared-leg bloomers or britches and proceed with the correct option below, starting with Rnd 7.

For Straight-Leg Bloomers

Rnd 7: Ch 3, dc in next st and in each st around; join TC with sl st in 3rd ch of beg ch-3 (30 dc).

Rnd 8: Ch 2, turn, working in blps only, hdc in next st and in each st around; join with sl st in 2nd ch of beg ch-2 (30 hdc).

Rnd 9: Ch 3, dc in next st and in each st around; join with sl st in 3rd ch of beg ch-3 (30 dc).

Rnd 10: Ch 2, hdc in next st and in each st around; join with sl st in 2nd ch of beg ch-2 (30 hdc).

Fasten off. Weave in ends. Fold pant cuff up.

For Flared-Leg Bloomers

Rnd 7: Ch 4, work 4 tr in same st as joining, * 5 tr in next st, rep from * around; join with sl st in 4th ch of beg ch-4 (150 tr).

Fasten off. Weave in ends.

For Straight-Leg Britches

Rnds 7–10: Ch 3, dc in next st and in each st around; join with sl st in 3rd ch of beg ch-3 (30 dc).

Rnd 11: Ch 3, dc in next st and in each st around; join TC with sl st in 3rd ch of beg ch-3 (30 dc).

Rnd 12: Ch 2, turn, working in blps only, hdc in next st and in each st around; join with sl st in 2nd ch of beg ch-2 (30 hdc).

Rnd 13: Ch 3, dc in next st and in each st around; join with sl st in 3rd ch of beg ch-3 (30 dc).

Rnd 14: Ch 2, hdc in next st and in each st around; join with sl st in 2nd ch of beg ch-2 (30 hdc).

Fasten off. Weave in ends. Fold pant cuff up.

For Flared-Leg Britches

Rnd 7: Ch 3, dc in same st as joining, dc in next dc, * 2 dc in next dc, dc in next dc, rep from * around; join with sl st in 3rd ch of beg ch-3 (45 dc).

Rnds 8–10: Ch 3, dc in next st and in each st around; join with sl st in 3rd ch of beg ch-3 (45 dc).

Rnd 11: Ch 4, work 4 tr in same st as joining, * 5 tr in next st, rep from * around; join with sl st in 4th ch of beg ch-4 (225 tr).

Fasten off. Weave in ends.

Leg Hole 2

With the top of the bloomers or britches facing you and the completed leg to the right, insert the hook directly through both dc (upper and lower) to the left of the completed leg (counts as one st); join MC.

Rnd 1: Ch 3, dc in same st as joining and in each st around to last st, 2 dc in last st; join with sl st in 3rd ch of beg ch-3 (30 dc).

Rnds 2–6: Ch 3, dc in next st and in each st around; join with sl st in 3rd ch of beg ch-3 (30 dc).

For Straight-Leg Bloomers

Work Rnds 7–10 the same as *Leg Hole 1 for Straight-Leg Bloomers*. Fasten off. Weave in ends. Fold pant cuff up.

For Flared-Leg Bloomers

Work Rnd 7 the same as *Leg Hole 1 for Flared-Leg Bloomers*. Fasten off. Weave in ends.

For Straight-Leg Britches

Work Rnds 7–14 the same as *Leg Hole 1 for Straight-Leg Britches.* Fasten off. Weave in ends. Fold pant cuff up.

For Flared-Leg Britches

Work Rnds 7–11 the same as *Leg Hole 1 for Flared-Leg Britches.* Fasten off. Weave in ends.

Bloomers & Britches (6–12 months)

Waistband

With MC, ch 66, being careful not to twist the ch; join with sl st in beg ch.

Rnd 1: Ch 2 (counts as hdc), hdc in next ch and in each ch around; join with sl st in 2nd ch of beg ch-2 (66 hdc).

Rnd 2: Ch 3 (counts as dc), dc in next st and in each st around; join with sl st in 3rd ch of beg ch-3 (66 dc).

Rnd 3: Ch 2, hdc in next st and in each st around; join MC with sl st in 2nd ch of beg ch-2 (66 hdc).

Rnds 4–15: Ch 3, dc in next st and in each st around; join with sl st in 3rd ch of beg ch-3 (66 dc).

Do not fasten off. Continue with *Leg Hole 1.*

Leg Hole 1

Rnd 1 (splitting of legs): Ch 3, dc in next 31 sts, (yo, insert hook in next dc and directly through dc to the left of beg ch-3 and proceed to finish dc), leaving rem 32 dc unworked; join with sl st in 3rd ch of beg ch-3 (33 dc).

Rnds 2–8: Ch 3, dc in next st and in each st around; join with sl st in 3rd ch of beg ch-3 (33 dc).

For Straight-Leg Bloomers

Rnd 9: Ch 3, dc in next st and in each st around; join TC with sl st in 3rd ch of beg ch-3 (33 dc).

Rnd 10: Ch 2, turn, working in blps only, hdc in next st and in each st around; join with sl st in 2nd ch of beg ch-2 (33 hdc).

Rnd 11: Ch 3, dc in next st and in each st around; join with sl st in 3rd ch of beg ch-3 (33 dc).

Rnd 12: Ch 2, hdc in next st and in each st around; join with sl st in 2nd ch of beg ch-2 (33 hdc).

Fasten off. Weave in end. Fold pant cuff up.

Add a Colored Waistband

Want to add a splash of color to your BLOOMERS & BRITCHES? Replace the main color yarn for the waistband with a complementary trim color, then join the main color on the last stitch of Round 3. See **Stitches & Techniques** for instructions on changing colors.

For Flared-Leg Bloomers

Rnd 9: Ch 4, work 4 tr in same st as joining, * 5 tr in next st, rep from * around; join with sl st in 4th ch of beg ch-4 (165 tr).

Fasten off. Weave in ends.

For Straight-Leg Britches

Rnd 9–12: Ch 3, dc in next st and in each st around; join with sl st in 3rd ch of beg ch-3 (33 dc).

Rnd 13: Ch 3, dc in next st and in each st around; join TC with sl st in 3rd ch of beg ch-3 (33 dc).

Rnd 14: Ch 2, turn, working in blps only, hdc in next st and in each st around; join with sl st in 2nd ch of beg ch-2 (33 hdc).

Rnd 15: Ch 3, dc in next st and in each st around; join with sl st in 3rd ch of beg ch-3 (33 dc).

Rnd 16: Ch 2, hdc in next st and in each st around; join with sl st in 2nd ch of beg ch-2 (33 hdc).

Fasten off. Weave in ends. Fold pant cuff up.

For Flared-Leg Britches

Rnd 9: Ch 3, dc in next st and in each st around; join with sl st in 3rd ch of beg ch-3 (33 dc).

Rnd 10: Ch 3, dc in same st as joining, * dc in next dc, 2 dc in next dc, rep from * around; join with sl st in 3rd ch of beg ch-3 (50 dc).

Rnds 11–13: Ch 3, dc in next st and in each st around; join with sl st in 3rd ch of beg ch-3 (50 dc).

Rnd 14: Ch 4, work 4 tr in same st as joining, * 5 tr in next st, rep from * around; join with sl st in 4th ch of beg ch-4 (250 tr).

Fasten off. Sew in ends.

Leg Hole 2

With the top of the bloomers or britches facing you and the completed leg to the right, insert the hook directly through both dc (upper and lower) to the left of the completed leg (counts as one st); join MC.

Rnd 1: Ch 3, dc in same st as joining and in each st around to last st, 2 dc in last st; join with sl st in 3rd ch of beg ch-3 (33 dc).

Rnds 2–8: Ch 3, dc in next st and in each st around; join with sl st in 3rd ch of beg ch-3 (33 dc).

For Straight-Leg Bloomers

Work Rnds 9–12 the same as *Leg Hole 1 for Straight-Leg Bloomers*. Fasten off. Weave in ends. Fold pant cuff up.

For Flared-Leg Bloomers

Work Rnd 9 the same as *Leg Hole 1 for Flared-Leg Bloomers*. Fasten off. Weave in ends.

For Straight-Leg Britches

Work Rnds 9–16 the same as *Leg Hole 1 for Straight-Leg Britches*. Fasten off. Weave in ends. Fold pant cuff up.

For Flared-Leg Britches

Work Rnds 9–14 the same as *Leg Hole 1 for Flared-Leg Britches*. Fasten off. Weave in ends.

Finishing Touches

Waist Tie

For 0–3 months (3–6 months, 6–12 months).

Using a yarn color of your choice, ch 121 (141, 161).

Row 1: Sc in 2nd ch from hook and in each ch across (120 [140, 160] sc).

Fasten off. Weave in ends.

Starting at the front-middle waist, weave one end of the tie, in and out, through the dc posts in Rnd 2 of the waistband and ending beside the beginning of the tie. Tie in a bow.

Knee Patch (optional)

Using an accent color of your choice, ch 9.

Row 1: Hdc in 2nd ch from hook, hdc in next ch and in each ch across (8 hdc).

Rows 2–6: Ch 2, turn, hdc in next st and in each st across (8 hdc).

Fasten off. Weave in ends.

Using the yarn color of your choice, thread the tapestry needle. Place the knee patch at an angle on the desired knee and whipstitch it into place.

Rear Bottom Flap (optional)

For sizes 0–3 months (3–6 months, 6–12 months).

Leaving a 20" (50.8cm) yarn tail, ch 21 (22, 23) with the TC.

Row 1: Dc in 4th ch from hook, dc in next ch and in each ch across (19 [20, 21] dc).

Row 2: Ch 3, turn, dc in next st and in each st across (19 [20, 21] dc).

Rows 3–6 (3–6) (3–7): Rep Row 2.

Fasten off. Weave in ends.

Using the 20" (50.8cm) tail left at the beginning, and making sure it is placed evenly in the middle, sew the bottom edge of the bottom flap onto the back of the bloomers or britches.

Using the rear bottom flap as a guide, sew a button onto the bloomers or britches under each upper corner of the flap. Attach the flap to a button at each corner.

Add Motifs to Your BLOOMERS & BRITCHES

Make a motif of your choice from Chapter 3 and sew it onto the knees or the bottom of the bloomers or britches.

Popping Chevron Blanket

This blanket is loads of fun, with stitches that pop and motifs that can be changed as your child grows. Start with puppies or kittens, then switch to rockets, monsters or owls as he or she gets older. If you would like the motifs to be permanent additions to your blanket, simply sew the motifs on. They can be easily removed and replaced later to give it a brand new look.

Since there is no gauge for this blanket, why not make one for yourself? Use worsted-weight yarn with a J hook to create a warm afghan and top it off with your favorite flower motifs on the corners.

MATERIALS

Sport weight yarn **3** in 3 colors of your choice

Color 1: 360 yds (329m)

Color 2: 360 yds (329m)

Color 3: 360 yds (329m)

Size I (5.5mm) crochet hook

⅞"–1" (2.2cm–2.5cm) buttons (one per motif)

Scissors

Tapestry needle

Finished Project Sizes

Approx. 36" × 46" (91.4cm × 116.8cm)

Gauge

No gauge required.

Glossary of Abbreviations

beg	beginning
ch(s)	chain(s)
dc	double crochet
dc dec	double crochet decrease
pc	popcorn stitch
prev	previous
rep	repeat
rnd(s)	round(s)
sk	skip
sl st	slip stitch
sp(s)	space(s)
st(s)	stitch(es)
()	work instructions within parentheses as many times as directed
C1	color 1
C2	color 2
C3	color 3

See **Stitches & Techniques** to learn the popcorn stitch (pc) and the double crochet decrease (dc dec).

Popping Chevron Blanket

With C1, ch 119.

Row 1: Dc in 4th ch from hook, dc in next 2 ch, (pc, ch 3, pc) in next st, dc in next 4 sts (chevron made), * sk next 3 ch, dc in next 4 ch, (pc, ch 3, pc) in next st, dc in next 4 sts, rep from * across (10 chevrons).

Row 2: Ch 3, turn, dc dec, dc in next 2 sts, (dc, ch 3, dc) in ch-3 sp, dc in next 4 dc, * sk next 2 sts, dc in next 4 sts, (dc, ch 3, dc) in ch-3 sp, dc in next 4 dc, rep from * across (10 chevrons).

Row 3: Ch 3, turn, dc dec, dc in next 2 sts, (pc, ch 3, pc) in ch-3 sp, dc in next 4 dc, * sk next 2 sts, dc in next 4 sts, (pc, ch 3, pc) in ch-3 sp, dc in next 4 dc, rep from * across (10 chevrons).

Row 4: Ch 3, turn, dc dec, dc in next 2 sts, (dc, ch 3, dc) in ch-3 sp, dc in next 4 dc, * sk next 2 sts, dc in next 4 sts, (dc, ch 3, dc) in ch-3 sp, dc in next 4 dc, rep from * across (10 chevrons).

Rows 5–7: Rep Rows 3 and 4, ending on Row 3.

Row 8: Ch 3, turn, dc dec, dc in next 2 sts, (dc, ch 3, dc) in ch-3 sp, dc in next 4 dc, * sk next 2 sts, dc in next 4 sts, (dc, ch 3, dc) in ch-3 sp, dc in next 4 dc, rep from * across, joining C2 in last dc (10 chevrons).

Row 9: Ch 3, turn, dc dec, dc in next 2 sts, (pc, ch 3, pc) in ch-3 sp, dc in next 4 dc, * sk next 2 sts, dc in next 4 sts, (pc, ch 3, pc) in ch-3 sp, dc in next 4 dc, rep from * across (10 chevrons).

Row 10: Ch 3, turn, dc dec, dc in next 2 sts, (dc, ch 3, dc) in ch-3 sp, dc in next 4 dc, * sk next 2 sts, dc in next 4 sts, (dc, ch 3, dc) in ch-3 sp, dc in next 4 dc, rep from * across (10 chevrons).

Rows 11–15: Rep Rows 9 and 10, ending on Row 9.

Row 16: Ch 3, turn, dc dec, dc in next 2 sts, (dc, ch 3, dc) in ch-3 sp, dc in next 4 dc, * sk next 2 sts, dc in next 4 sts, (dc, ch 3, dc) in ch-3 sp, dc in next 4 dc, rep from * across, joining C3 in last dc (10 chevrons).

Row 17: Ch 3, turn, dc dec, dc in next 2 sts, (pc, ch 3, pc) in ch-3 sp, dc in next 4 dc, * sk next 2 sts, dc in next 4 sts, (pc, ch 3, pc) in ch-3 sp, dc in next 4 dc, rep from * across (10 chevrons).

Row 18: Ch 3, turn, dc dec, dc in next 2 sts, (dc, ch 3, dc) in ch-3 sp, dc in next 4 dc, * sk next 2 sts, dc in next 4 sts, (dc, ch 3, dc) in ch-3 sp, dc in next 4 dc, rep from * across (10 chevrons).

Rows 19–23: Rep Rows 17 and 18, ending on Row 17.

Row 24: Ch 3, turn, dc dec, dc in next 2 sts, (dc, ch 3, dc) in ch-3 sp, dc in next 4 dc, * sk next 2 sts, dc in next 4 sts, (dc, ch 3, dc) in ch-3 sp, dc in next 4 dc, rep from * across, joining C1 in last dc st (10 chevrons).

Row 25: Ch 3, turn, dc dec, dc in next 2 sts, (pc, ch 3, pc) in ch-3 sp, dc in next 4 dc, * sk next 2 sts, dc in next 4 sts, (pc, ch 3, pc) in ch-3 sp, dc in next 4 dc, rep from * across (10 chevrons).

Row 26: Ch 3, turn, dc dec, dc in next 2 sts, (dc, ch 3, dc) in ch-3 sp, dc in next 4 dc, * sk next 2 sts, dc in next 4 sts, (dc, ch 3, dc) in ch-3 sp, dc in next 4 dc, rep from * across (10 chevrons).

Row 27–31: Rep Rows 25 and 26, ending on Row 25.

Row 32: Ch 3, turn, dc dec, dc in next 2 sts, (dc, ch 3, dc) in ch-3 sp, dc in next 4 dc, * sk next 2 sts, dc in next 4 sts, (dc, ch 3, dc) in ch-3 sp, dc in next 4 dc, rep from * across, joining C2 in last dc (10 chevrons).

Rows 33–71: Rep Rows 9–32, ending on Row 23.

Row 72: Ch 3, turn, dc dec, dc in next 2 sts, (dc, ch 3, dc) in ch-3 sp, dc in next 4 dc, * sk next 2 sts, dc in next 4 sts, (dc, ch 3, dc) in ch-3 sp, dc in next 4 dc, rep from * across, joining C2 in last dc (10 chevrons).

Do not fasten off.

Blanket Trim

Rnd 1: With C2 joined (see Row 72), ch 2, turn, work 2 hdc in same st as joining, hdc across top of blanket making sure to sk the 2 skipped sts from the prev row and working 3 hdc in each of the 2nd chs of the ch-3 chevron points, 3 hdc in corner st, hdc in next st and in each st across to corner, work 3 hdc in corner st, hdc across bottom of blanket making sure to sk the skipped sts from the prev row and working 3 hdc in each of the 2nd chs of the ch-3 chevron points, 3 hdc in corner st, hdc in next st and in each st across to corner, join C1 with sl st in 2nd ch of beg ch-2.

Rnd 2: Ch 2, hdc in each st around, working 3 hdc in each of the 2nd hdc corner sts and in each of the 2nd hdc chevron point sts and sk each of the skipped sts in the prev rnd, join C3 with sl st in 2nd ch of beg ch-2.

Rnd 3: Ch 2, hdc in each st around, working 3 hdc in each 2nd hdc corner st and in each of the 2nd hdc chevron point sts and sk each of the skipped sts in the prev rnd; join with sl st in 2nd ch of beg ch-2.

Fasten off. Weave in ends.

Finishing Touches

To complete your Popping Chevron Blanket, make as many motifs from Chapter 3 as you choose and sew buttons onto the blanket where you would like the motifs placed. If you prefer, make the crochet button alternative at the beginning of the book instead of using hard buttons, then attach the motifs to the blanket.

This blanket can be made larger or smaller by adding or decreasing in multiples of 12 stitches.

12 sts = 1 chevron

Shoulder Pack

I designed the SHOULDER PACK with comfort in mind, so I made the strap adjustable and wide to be gentle on the shoulder. With the drawstring and button closures, it's sure to be a hit! Make them for boys or girls in their favorite colors. Kids will love mixing up the motifs on the front of the SHOULDER PACK to give each one its own look.

MATERIALS

Worsted weight yarn **(4)** in the color of your choice (360 yds/329m)

Size J (6mm) crochet hook

⅞"–1" (2.2cm–2.5cm) buttons (6 for the pack, plus 1 for each motif)

Scissors

Stitch markers

Tapestry needle

Finished Project Sizes

3½" wide × 10" long × 12½" high (8.9cm × 25.4cm × 31.8cm), unstretched

Gauge

7 sts = 2" (5.1cm)

4 rows hdc = 2" (5.1cm)

Glossary of Abbreviations

beg	beginning
bpdc	back post double crochet
bphdc	back post half double crochet
ch(s)	chain(s)
fphdc	front post half double crochet
hdc	half double crochet
rep	repeat
rnd(s)	round(s)
sl st	slip stitch
st(s)	stitch(es)

Shoulder Pack

Ch 21.

Rnd 1: Work 2 hdc in 3rd ch from hook, hdc in next 17 chs, 3 hdc in last ch; working around the other side of ch, work hdc in next 17 sts; join with sl st in 2nd ch of beg ch-2 (40 hdc).

Rnd 2: Ch 2, hdc in same st as joining, 2 hdc in next 4 sts, hdc in next 14 sts, 2 hdc in next 6 sts, hdc in next 14 sts, 2 hdc in last st; join with sl st in 2nd ch of beg ch-2 (52 hdc).

Rnd 3: Ch 2, 2 hdc in next 8 sts, hdc in next 18 sts, 2 hdc in next 8 sts, hdc in last 17 sts; join with sl st in 2nd ch of beg ch-2 (68 hdc).

Rnd 4: Ch 2, hdc in next 4 sts, 2 hdc in next 8 sts, hdc in next 26 sts, 2 hdc in next 8 sts, hdc in last 21 sts; join with sl st in 2nd ch of beg ch-2 (84 hdc).

Rnds 5–6: Ch 2, bpdc in next st and in each st around, join with sl st in 2nd ch of beg ch-2 (84 sts).

Rnds 7–8: Ch 2, hdc in next st and in each st around; join with sl st in 2nd ch of beg ch-2 (84 hdc).

Rnds 9–10: Ch 2, bpdc in next st and in each st around; join with sl st in 2nd ch of beg ch-2 (84 sts).

Rnds 11–12: Ch 2, hdc in next st and in each st around; join with sl st in 2nd ch of beg ch-2 (84 hdc).

Rnds 13–14: Ch 2, bpdc in next st and in each st around; join with sl st in 2nd ch of beg ch-2 (84 sts).

Rnds 15–16: Ch 2, hdc in next st and in each st around; join with sl st in 2nd ch of beg ch-2 (84 hdc).

Rnds 17–18: Ch 2, bpdc in next st and in each st around; join with sl st in 2nd ch of beg ch-2 (84 sts).

Rnds 19–20: Ch 2, hdc in next st and in each st around; join with sl st in 2nd ch of beg ch-2 (84 hdc).

Rnds 21–22: Ch 2, bpdc in next st and in each st around; join with sl st in 2nd ch of beg ch-2 (84 sts).

Rnds 23–24: Ch 2, hdc in next st and in each st around; join with sl st in 2nd ch of beg ch-2 (84 hdc).

Rnds 25–26: Ch 2, bpdc in next st and in each st around; join with sl st in 2nd ch of beg ch-2 (84 sts).

Rnds 27–28: Ch 2, hdc in next st and in each st around; join with sl st in 2nd ch of beg ch-2 (84 hdc).

Rnds 29–30: Ch 2, bpdc in next st and in each st around; join with sl st in 2nd ch of beg ch-2 (84 sts).

Rnds 31–32: Ch 2, hdc in next st and in each st around; join with sl st in 2nd ch of beg ch-2 (84 hdc).

Rnds 33–34: Ch 2, bpdc in next st and in each st around; join with sl st in 2nd ch of beg ch-2 (84 sts).

Rnds 35–36: Ch 2, hdc in next st and in each st around; join with sl st in 2nd ch of beg ch-2 (84 hdc).

Rnd 37: Ch 2, bpdc in next st and in each st around; join with sl st in 2nd ch of beg ch-2 (84 sts).

Rnd 38: Ch 2, bphdc in next 6 sts, bphdc in next st (place a st marker around the post of this st; st markers will be used for the shoulder strap), bphdc in each st around to last 2 sts, bphdc in next st (place a st marker around the post of this st), bphdc in last st; join with sl st in 2nd ch of beg ch-2 (84 sts).

Rnd 39: Ch 2, hdc in next st and in each st around; join with sl st in 2nd ch of beg ch-2 (84 hdc).

Rnd 40: Ch 1, sl st in same st as joining and in each st around; join with sl st in beg ch-1 (84 sl sts).

Fasten off. Weave in ends. Do not turn SHOULDER PACK, join yarn with sl st in the 6th to last sl st worked to begin the *Shoulder Pack Flap*.

Shoulder Pack Flap

Row 1: Ch 2; working in the sl sts, hdc in next st and in next 21 sts (23 hdc).

Row 2: Ch 2, turn, fphdc in next st and in each st across to last st, hdc in last st (23 sts).

Row 3: Ch 2, turn, bphdc in next st and in each st across to last st, hdc in last st (23 sts).

Rows 4–5: Ch 2, turn, hdc in next st and in each st across (23 hdc).

Rows 6–12: Rep Rows 2–5, ending on Row 4.

Row 13: Ch 1, turn, sl st in next st and in each st across (22 sl sts).

Fasten off. Weave in ends.

Rows can easily be added to the Shoulder Strap as your child grows. Just undo the ending knot, join yarn and add as many rows as needed.

Shoulder Strap

With the front of the pack facing down and the top of the pack towards you, insert the hook around the post of the right st marker; join yarn with a sl st.

Row 1: Ch 2, hdc around post of next st and in each st across to the other st marker (once row is complete, remove st markers) (10 hdc).

Row 2: Ch 2, turn, hdc in next st and in each st across (10 hdc).

Row 3: Ch 2, turn, bpdc in next st and in each st across to last st, hdc in last st (10 sts).

Row 4: Ch 2, turn, fpdc in next st and in each st across to last st, hdc in last st (10 sts).

Rows 5–6: Ch 2, turn, hdc in next st and in each st across (10 hdc).

Rows 7–62: Rep Rows 3–6.

Row 63: Ch 1, sl st in 1st st and in each st across (10 sl sts).

Fasten off. Weave in ends.

Next, with the back of the SHOULDER PACK facing you (bottom toward you), sew 3 buttons onto the 1st, 5th and 10th hdc post to the left of the Rnd 6 joining seam. These 3 buttons will be used to attach the bottom of the adjustable strap.

Button the strap onto the buttons using the 2nd to last hdc row. If you choose to make the strap permanent, ch 1, turn, sl st through each st of the strap and directly through to the corresponding 10 post sts to the right of the Rnd 5 joining seam and fasten off. Another alternative is to fasten off after the last row of the strap and sew the strap onto the above sts.

If the strap is too short, unbutton it, take out the joining knot, join the yarn and continue with the pattern until you reach the desired length.

Backpack Tie

Using 2 strands of yarn, ch 110.

Fasten off.

Working in top hdc round of SHOULDER PACK

Starting at the middle-front of the SHOULDER PACK opening, weave one end of the tie in and out through the dc posts in the 2nd rnd from the top and end beside the beg of the tie. Tighten and tie in a bow to close the SHOULDER PACK.

Once the ties are tied, fold the flap over to measure where to sew the buttons onto the SHOULDER PACK. The buttons should be sewn under the last hdc row of the flap. Sew 3 buttons onto the SHOULDER PACK, one for each corner and one in the middle. Once the buttons are sewn on, use the last hdc row of the flap to button onto the buttons.

Finishing Touches

To complete your SHOULDER PACK, make motifs of your choice from Chapter 3 and sew buttons anywhere on the front of the pack. Attach the motifs to the buttons. If you would like to use the motifs as a permanent addition to your pack, you may sew them on. They can be easily removed and replaced with new ones if you would like a change later.

To wear the SHOULDER PACK, place your right arm and head through the shoulder strap and adjust it to rest diagonally across your body.

Tic-Tac-Toe Travel Game

EASY/INTERMEDIATE

Want to keep the kids busy on those long car trips? This TIC-TAC-TOE TRAVEL GAME is sure to pass the time! Whip one up, then choose two of your favorite accents from Chapter 3 to use as the game pieces. When they're done playing, put the game pieces into the open side pouch of the game board, roll it and tie it up. It's easy and convenient!

MATERIALS

Sport weight yarn **3** in 4 colors of your choice

Color 1: 82 yds (75m)

Color 2: 72 yds (66m)

Color 3: 86 yds (79m)

Border color: 94 yds (86m)

Size I (5.5mm) crochet hook

Nine ⅞"–1" (2.2cm–2.5cm) buttons

Scissors

Tapestry needle

Finished Project Sizes

13" × 12½" (33cm × 31.8cm)

Gauge

No gauge required.

Glossary of Abbreviations

beg	beginning
ch(s)	chain(s)
dc	double crochet
hdc	half double crochet
rnd(s)	round(s)
RS	right side
sc	single crochet
sk	skip
sl st	slip stitch
sp(s)	space(s)
st(s)	stitch(es)
rep	repeat
WS	wrong side
yo	yarn over
*	repeat instructions following the asterisk as directed
( )	work instructions within parentheses as many times as directed
C1	color 1
C2	color 2
C3	color 3
BC	border color

Tic-Tac-Toe Game Board

Square A (make 5)

With C1, ch 5; join with sl st in beg ch to form ring.

Rnd 1: Ch 3, work 15 dc in ring; join with sl st in 3rd ch of beg ch-3 (16 dc).

Rnd 2: Ch 1, sc in same st as joining, ch 2, * sk next st, sc in next st, ch 2, rep from * around; join with sl st in beg sc (8 ch-2 sps).

Fasten off.

Rnd 3: Join C2 in any ch-2 sp, (ch 2, 2 hdc, ch 2, 3 hdc) in same ch-2 sp as joining, 3 hdc in next ch-2 sp, * (3 hdc, ch 2, 3 hdc) in next ch-2 sp, 3 hdc in next ch-2 sp, rep from * around; join with sl st in 2nd ch of beg ch-2 (36 hdc, 4 ch-2 sps).

Fasten off.

Rnd 4: Join C3 in any ch-2 sp, (ch 3, 2 dc, ch 2, 3 dc) in same ch-2 sp as joining, dc in next 8 sts, * (3 dc, ch 2, 3 dc) in next ch-2 sp, dc in next 8 sts, rep from * around; join with sl st in 3rd ch of beg ch-3 (56 dc).

Fasten off. Weave in ends.

Square B (make 4)

With C3, ch 5; join with sl st in beg ch to form ring.

Rnd 1: Ch 3, work 15 dc in ring; join with sl st in 3rd ch of beg ch-3 (16 dc).

Rnd 2: Ch 1, sc in same st as joining, ch 2, * sk next st, sc in next st, ch 2, rep from * around; join with sl st in beg sc (8 ch-2 sps).

Fasten off.

Rnd 3: Join C2 in any ch-2 sp, (ch 2, 2 hdc, ch 2, 3 hdc) in same ch-2 sp as joining, 3 hdc in next ch-2 sp, * (3 hdc, ch 2, 3 hdc) in next ch-2 sp, 3 hdc in next ch-2 sp, rep from * around; join with sl st in 2nd ch of beg ch-2 (36 hdc, 4 ch-2 sps).

Fasten off.

Rnd 4: Join C1 in any ch-2 sp, (ch 3, 2 dc, ch 2, 3 dc) in same ch-2 sp as joining, dc in next 8 sts, * (3 dc, ch 2, 3 dc) in next ch-2 sp, dc in next 8 sts, rep from * around; join with sl st in 3rd ch of beg ch-3 (56 dc).

Fasten off. Weave in ends.

Placement of the Granny Squares

You will first have to lay the squares out to make the board.

Using the diagram, place the 5 Square A pieces in the 1, 3, 5, 7 and 9 positions.

Next, place the 4 Square B pieces in the 2, 4, 6 and 8 positions.

Joining the Granny Squares Together

1	2	3
4	5	6
7	8	9

First Seams

Starting with the bottom 2 rows of squares, and working from right to left, place squares 6 and 9 together (square 9 facing you, square 6 toward the back) with WS together.

Working through both loops on both pieces:

Insert hook in the ch-2 corner sp and join BC, ch 1, sc in same ch-2 sp as joining and in next 14 sts, then sc in the ch-2 sp of the next corner. Do not fasten off.

Place squares 5 and 8 (beside squares 6 and 9), with WS together. Insert the hook in the ch-2 corner sp and sc, sc in next 14 sts, then sc in the ch-2 sp of the next corner. Do not fasten off.

Place squares 4 and 7 (beside squares 5 and 8), with WS together. Insert the hook in the ch-2 corner sp and sc, sc in next 14 sts, then sc in the ch-2 sp of the next corner. Fasten off.

Next, place square 3 behind square 6 (WS together) and insert hook through the ch-2 corner sp of square 6 and then the ch-2 corner sp of square 3; join BC, ch 1, sc in same ch-2 sp as joining and in next 14 sts, then sc in the ch-2 sp of the next corner. Do not fasten off.

Place square 2 behind square 5 (WS together) and insert hook through the ch-2 corner sp of square 5 and then the ch-2 corner sp of square 2 and sc, sc in next 14 sts, then sc in the ch-2 sp of the next corner. Do not fasten off.

Place square 1 behind square 4 (WS together) and insert hook through the ch-2 corner sp of square 4 and then the ch-2 corner sp of square 1 and sc, sc in next 14 sts, then sc in the ch-2 sp of the next corner.

Fasten off.

Blend the joining seams of the squares into the outer border round

When you are working the sc around the outer border and come to the sc joining seams of the squares, insert hook (from right to left) through the last joining seam sc and directly into the next ch-2 sp, yo and proceed with sc. Doing this creates a clean line instead of making the seams appear separated from the border.

Alternate Seams

Next, turn the game board one rotation to the right or left and sc the alternate seam lengths together by inserting the hook in the beg ch-2 corner sp, joining BC, ch 1 and sc in same ch-2 sp as joining, then sc in each st and ch-2 sp across, ending with a sc in the last ch-2 sp. Fasten off. Repeat for the other seam.

Outer Border

Join BC in any ch-2 corner st, ch 1, work 3 sc in same ch-2 sp as joining, continue to sc in each st and ch-2 sp around, working 3 sc in each of the last 3 ch-2 sp corners; join with sl st in beg sc.

Once the border is complete, sew one button onto the center of each square (9 buttons).

Diagonal Back Piece of Game Board

With C1, ch 6.

Row 1: Dc in 4th ch from hook, dc in last 2 ch (block made) (4 dc,1 block).

Row 2: Ch 6, turn, dc in 4th ch from hook, dc in last 2 ch, (sk next 3 dc, sl st, ch 3, 3 dc) in next ch-3 sp (8 dc, 2 blocks).

Row 3: Ch 6, turn, dc in 4th ch from hook, dc in last 2 ch, * sk next 3 dc, (sl st, ch 3, 3 dc) in next ch-3 sp, rep from * across (12 dc, 3 blocks).

Row 4: Ch 6, turn, dc in 4th ch from hook, dc in last 2 ch, * sk next 3 dc, (sl st, ch 3, 3 dc) in next ch-3 sp, rep from * across changing color on last dc to C2 (16 dc, 4 blocks).

Row 5: Ch 6, turn, dc in 4th ch from hook, dc in last 2 ch, * sk next 3 dc, (sl st, ch 3, 3 dc) in next ch-3 sp, rep from * across (20 dc, 5 blocks).

Row 6: Ch 6, turn, dc in 4th ch from hook, dc in last 2 ch, * sk next 3 dc, (sl st, ch 3, 3 dc) in next ch-3 sp, rep from * across (24 dc, 6 blocks).

Row 7: Ch 6, turn, dc in 4th ch from hook, dc in last 2 ch, * sk next 3 dc, (sl st, ch 3, 3 dc) in next ch-3 sp, rep from * across (28 dc, 7 blocks).

Row 8: Ch 6, turn, dc in 4th ch from hook, dc in last 2 ch, * sk next 3 dc, (sl st, ch 3, 3 dc) in next ch-3 sp, rep from * across changing color on last dc to C3 (32 dc, 8 blocks).

Row 9: Ch 6, turn, dc in 4th ch from hook, dc in last 2 ch, * sk next 3 dc, (sl st, ch 3, 3 dc) in next ch-3 sp, rep from * across (36 dc, 9 blocks).

Row 10: Ch 6, turn, dc in 4th ch from hook, dc in last 2 ch, * sk next 3 dc, (sl st, ch 3, 3 dc) in next ch-3 sp, rep from * across (40 dc, 10 blocks).

Row 11: Ch 6, turn, dc in 4th ch from hook, dc in last 2 ch, * sk next 3 dc, (sl st, ch 3, 3 dc) in next ch-3 sp, rep from * across (44 dc, 11 blocks).

Row 12: Ch 6, turn, dc in 4th ch from hook, dc in last 2 ch, * sk next 3 dc, (sl st, ch 3, 3 dc) in next ch-3 sp, rep from * across changing color on last dc to BC (48 dc, 12 blocks).

Row 13: Ch 6, turn, dc in 4th ch from hook, dc in last 2 ch, * sk next 3 dc, (sl st, ch 3, 3 dc) in next ch-3 sp, rep from * across (52 dc, 13 blocks).

Row 14: Ch 6, turn, dc in 4th ch from hook, dc in last 2 ch, * sk next 3 dc, (sl st, ch 3, 3 dc) in next ch-3 sp, rep from * across (56 dc, 14 blocks).

Row 15: Ch 6, turn, dc in 4th ch from hook, dc in last 2 ch, * sk next 3 dc, (sl st, ch 3, 3 dc) in next ch-3 sp, rep from * across (60 dc, 15 blocks).

Row 16: Turn, do not ch, sl st in next 3 sts, (sl st, ch 3, 3 dc) in next ch-3 sp, * sk next 3 dc, (sl st, ch 3, 3 dc) in next ch-3 sp, rep from * across to last block; sk next 3 dc, sl st in last ch-3 sp (56 dc, 14 blocks).

Row 17: Turn, do not ch, sl st in next 3 sts, (sl st, ch 3, 3 dc) in next ch-3 sp, * sk next 3 dc, (sl st, ch 3, 3 dc) in next ch-3 sp, rep from * across to last block; sk next 3 dc, sl st in last ch-3 sp (52 dc, 13 blocks).

Row 18: Turn, do not ch, sl st in next 3 sts, (join C1 with sl st, ch 3, 3 dc) in next ch-3 sp, * sk next 3 dc, (sl st, ch 3, 3 dc) in next ch-3 sp, rep from * across to last block; sk next 3 dc, sl st in last ch-3 sp (48 dc, 12 blocks).

Row 19: Turn, do not ch, sl st in next 3 sts, (sl st, ch 3, 3 dc in next ch-3 sp, * sk next 3 dc, (sl st, ch 3, 3 dc) in next ch-3 sp, rep from * across to last block; sk next 3 dc, sl st in last ch-3 sp (44 dc, 11 blocks).

Row 20: Turn, do not ch, sl st in next 3 sts, (sl st, ch 3, 3 dc) in next ch-3 sp, * sk next 3 dc, (sl st, ch 3, 3 dc) in next ch-3 sp, rep from * across to last block, sk next 3 dc, sl st in last ch-3 sp (40 dc, 10 blocks).

Row 21: Turn, do not ch, sl st in next 3 sts, (sl st, ch 3, 3 dc) in next ch-3 sp, * sk next 3 dc, (sl st, ch 3, 3 dc) in next ch-3 sp, rep from * across to last block; sk next 3 dc, sl st in last ch-3 sp (36 dc, 9 blocks).

Row 22: Turn, do not ch, sl st in next 3 sts, (join C2 with sl st, ch 3, 3 dc) in next ch-3 sp, * sk next 3 dc, (sl st, ch 3, 3 dc) in next ch-3 sp, rep from * across to last block; sk next 3 dc, sl st in last ch-3 sp (32 dc, 8 blocks).

Row 23: Turn, do not ch, sl st in next 3 sts, (sl st, ch 3, 3 dc) in next ch-3 sp, * sk next 3 dc, (sl st, ch 3, 3 dc) in next ch-3 sp, rep from * across to last block; sk next 3 dc, sl st in last ch-3 sp (28 dc, 7 blocks).

Row 24: Turn, do not ch, sl st in next 3 sts, (sl st, ch 3, 3 dc) in next ch-3 sp, * sk next 3 dc, (sl st, ch 3, 3 dc) in next ch-3 sp, rep from * across to last block; sk next 3 dc, sl st in last ch-3 sp (24 dc, 6 blocks).

Row 25: Turn, do not ch, sl st in next 3 sts, (sl st, ch 3, 3 dc) in next ch-3 sp, * sk next 3 dc, (sl st, ch 3, 3 dc) in next ch-3 sp, rep from * across to last block, sk next 3 dc, sl st in last ch-3 sp (20 dc, 5 blocks).

Row 26: Turn, do not ch, sl st in next 3 sts, (join C3 with sl st, ch 3, 3 dc) in next ch-3 sp, * sk next 3 dc, (sl st, ch 3, 3 dc) in next ch-3 sp, rep from * across to last block, sk next 3 dc, sl st in last ch-3 sp (16 dc, 4 blocks).

Row 27: Turn, do not ch, sl st in next 3 sts, (sl st, ch 3, 3 dc) in next ch-3 sp, * sk next 3 dc, (sl st, ch 3, 3 dc) in next ch-3 sp, rep from * across to last block; sk next 3 dc, sl st in last ch-3 sp (12 dc, 3 blocks).

Row 28: Turn, do not ch, sl st in next 3 sts, (sl st, ch 3, 3 dc) in next ch-3 sp, * sk next 3 dc, (sl st, ch 3, 3 dc) in next ch-3 sp, rep from * across to last block; sk next 3 dc, sl st in last ch-3 sp (8 dc, 2 blocks).

Row 29: Turn, do not ch, sl st in next 3 sts, (sl st, ch 3, 3 dc) in next ch-3 sp; sk next 3 dc, sl st in the last ch-3 sp (4 dc, 1 block).

Fasten off. Weave in all ends.

Diagonal Back Piece Outer Border

Join BC in any corner sp, (ch 1, sc, 2 hdc) in same sp as joining, work 44 hdc evenly across; next, work (2 hdc, sc) in corner sp, work 44 sc evenly across; next, work (sc, 2 hdc) in corner sp, work 44 hdc evenly across, then work (2 hdc, sc) in corner sp; finally, work 44 sc evenly across, join with sl st in beg sc.

Joining Board Side and Back Side Together

With WS together, work through both loops of both pieces. Insert the hook in any 2nd st of corner st and join BC, sl st in the next st and in each st around 3 sides. Leave the last side open (this opening will hold the game pieces). Fasten off and weave in ends.

Ties (make 3)

Holding any 2 colors together, ch 90. Fasten off.

On the side (opposite the open side), thread a tie through the center of the sl st border trim in each of the 3 squares. Pull the tie halfway through so both ends are even and tie a knot at the center to secure (the ends of the ties should remain separate so that they can be tied together when the board is rolled up).

To Wrap Board Game

With the open edge of the game facing you (bottom edge with ties away from you), place the game pieces evenly spaced out and flat in the pouch, then roll the game into a tube, wrap the ends of each tie around the tube and tie them in a bow.

Game Pieces

Choose any 2 motifs from Chapter 3 and make 5 of each. Use these as the game pieces by buttoning and unbuttoning them on the game board. Place the game pieces into the open end of the game board to store them.

 If you're slip stitching the board and back sides together, and the squares are not exactly even with one another, don't fret.

If there are too few stitches on the bottom piece, insert the hook in the next stitch (through the top piece only), then insert the hook through the slip stitch you just made (through the bottom piece only), yarn over and slip stitch. This will add a slip stitch to the bottom piece but not to the top piece. Continue until both pieces are even, then resume slip stitching through both pieces.

If you have too few stitches on the top piece, insert the hook in the slip stitch just made (through top piece only), then insert the hook through the next unworked stitch (through bottom piece only), yarn over and slip stitch. This will add a slip stitch to the top but not to the bottom. Continue until both pieces are even, then resume slip stitching through both pieces.

Chapter 2
Fun for Adults

I wanted to make some practical yet trendy items that we adults could use in our everyday lives. Designs so great that we can't wait to share by making them as gifts for our family and friends. Well, these five patterns are fabulous!

The BOHO SHRUG has a short-sleeve and a long-sleeve version, and it looks amazing on. The FRILLED LEG WARMERS and the WAVY COWL can be worn with any outfit, dressy or casual. The SCALLOPED FINGERLESS GLOVES are perfect for keeping your arms and hands warm while texting or working on the computer, and the LARGE MARKET BAG is a definite must-have! It's perfect for groceries, crochet projects or managing your beach gear!

Boho Shrug

You don't have to worry about being chilly during those cool days when you have this gorgeous shrug on. These shrugs are cozy like a big warm hug! Crocheted in one piece while working the same stitches for the sleeves and the back creates two unique textures, and the rows of big bobbles on the sleeves definitely gives it that boho feel. Add your favorite motif or a big chunky wooden button on the collar. Choose the short sleeve or the long sleeve version.

MATERIALS

Short sleeve shrug: Sport weight yarn [3] in the color of your choice (1,127 yds/1,031m)

Long sleeve shrug: Sport weight yarn [3] in the color of your choice (1,368 yds/1,251m)

Size J (6mm) crochet hook

Scissors

Tapestry needle

⁷/₈"–1" (2.2cm–2.5cm) button

Finished Project Sizes

Short sleeve shrug: 43" (109.2cm) long

Long sleeve shrug: 60" (152.4cm) long

Gauge

11 sts = 3" (7.6cm)

5 rows dc = 3" (7.6cm)

Glossary of Abbreviations

beg	beginning
ch(s)	chain(s)
dc	double crochet
hdc	half double crochet
rep	repeat
rnd(s)	round(s)
st(s)	stitch(es)
sl st	slip stitch
tr	treble crochet
trbs	treble crochet bobble stitch
*	repeat instructions following the asterisk as directed
()	work instructions within the parentheses as many times as directed

To measure, hold arms straight out in front. Measure from one wrist, up the arm, around the back and down the other arm to the other wrist.

See **Stitches & Techniques** to learn the treble crochet bobble stitch (trbs).

Boho Shrug

Ch 80, being careful not to twist the ch; join with sl st in beg ch.

Sleeve

Rnd 1: Ch 2 (counts as hdc), hdc in next ch and in each ch around; join with sl st in 2nd ch of beg ch-2 (80 hdc).

Rnd 2: Ch 3 (counts as dc), dc in next 2 sts, trbs in next st, * dc in next 3 sts, trbs in next st, rep from * around; join with sl st in 3rd ch of beg ch-3 (60 dc, 20 trbs).

Rnd 3: Ch 2, hdc in next st and in each st around; join with sl st in 2nd ch of beg ch-2 (80 hdc).

Rnds 4–9: Rep Rnds 2 and 3.

Rnd 10: Ch 2, tr in next st, * hdc in next st, tr in next st, rep from * around; join with sl st in 2nd ch of beg ch-2 (80 sts).

Rnd 11: Ch 3, hdc in next tr, * tr in next hdc, hdc in next tr, rep from * around; join with sl st in 3rd ch of beg ch-3 (80 sts).

For Short Sleeves

Rnds 12–21: Rep Rnds 10 and 11.

Do not fasten off. Continue with Row 1 of *Back*.

For Long Sleeves

Rnds 12–31: Rep Rnds 10 and 11.

Do not fasten off. Continue with Row 1 of *Back*.

Back

Row 1: Ch 2, tr in next hdc, * hdc in next tr, tr in next hdc, rep from * across to last st; do not join with sl st (80 sts).

Row 2: Ch 2, turn, tr in next hdc, * hdc in next tr, tr in next hdc, rep from * across (80 sts).

Rows 3–37: Rep Row 2.

Do not turn. Do not fasten off. Lay shrug flat and fold ends closest to your hook together to form the 2nd sleeve, making sure they are folded in the same direction as the 1st sleeve.

Second Sleeve Hole

Join with sl st in 2nd ch of beg ch-2 of Row 37.

Rnd 1: Ch 3, hdc in next tr,* tr in next hdc, hdc in next tr, rep from * around; join with sl st in 3rd ch of beg ch-3 (80 sts).

Rnd 2: Ch 2, tr in next hdc, * hdc in next tr, tr in next hdc, rep from * around; join with sl st in 2nd ch of beg ch-2 (80 sts).

For Short Sleeves

Rnds 3–12: Rep Rnds 1 and 2.

Do not fasten off, continue below with Rnd 23.

For Long Sleeves

Rnds 3–22: Rep Rnds 1 and 2.

Do not fasten off. Continue below with Rnd 23.

Rnd 23: Ch 2, hdc in next st and in each st around; join with sl st in 2nd ch of beg ch-2 (80 hdc).

Rnd 24: Ch 3, dc in next 2 hdc, trbs in next hdc, * dc in next 3 hdc, trbs in next hdc, rep from * around; join with sl st in 3rd ch of beg ch-3 (60 dc, 20 trbs).

Rnds 25–31: Rep Rnds 23 and 24, ending on Rnd 23.

Fasten off. Weave in ends.

Trim around inner circle opening (neck or waist)

With the RS of the shrug facing you, join the yarn with a sl st in any st around the opening.

Rnd 1: Ch 2, work 159 hdc evenly around opening; join with sl st in 2nd ch of beg ch-2 (160 hdc).

Rnds 2–3: Ch 2, hdc in next st and in each st around; join with sl st in 2nd ch of beg ch-2 (160 hdc).

Fasten off. Weave in ends.

Finishing Touches

For button placement, put the shrug on and weave a scrap piece of yarn through the collar where you would like the motif to be placed. Remove the shrug and sew the button to the marked location. Be sure to remove the scrap yarn before you begin sewing.

Attach your favorite motif from Chapter 3 to the button.

Frilled Leg Warmers

Looking for the perfect pair of leg warmers that will look great with skirts and dresses and also over your favorite pair of yoga pants? Then, look no further! These FRILLED LEG WARMERS are trendy and fashionable. The generous length also allows them to fit over your favorite boots, too. Just unbutton a few buttons on the bottom, and they will look fabulous!

MATERIALS

Sport weight yarn (3) in 2 colors of your choice

Main Color: 642 yds (587m)

Trim: 27 yds (25m)

Size H (5mm) crochet hook

Size I (5.5mm) crochet hook

Twenty-eight ⅞"–1" (2.2cm–2.5cm) buttons

Scissors

Tapestry needle

Finished Project Sizes

One Size: 13" circumference × 19" long, unstretched (33cm × 48.3cm)

Gauge

15 sts = 4" (10.2cm)

7 rows dc = 4" (10.2cm)

Glossary of Abbreviations

beg	beginning		st(s)	stitch(es)
bpdc	back post double crochet		tr	treble crochet
bphdc	back post half double crochet		*	repeat instructions following the asterisk as directed
ch(s)	chain(s)		( )	work instructions within the parentheses as many times as directed
dc	double crochet			
fpdc	front post double crochet			
fphdc	front post half double crochet		MC	main color
			TC	trim color
hdc	half double crochet			
prev	previous			
rep	repeat			
rnd(s)	round(s)			
RS	right side			
sc	single crochet			
sk	skip			
sl st	slip stitch			
sp(s)	space(s)			

Frilled Leg Warmers

With I hook and MC, ch 70.

Row 1: Hdc in 3rd ch from hook and in each ch across (69 hdc).

Row 2 (RS): Ch 2, turn, fphdc around next 2 sts, * bphdc around next 3 sts, fphdc around next 2 sts, rep from * to last st; hdc in last st (69 hdc).

Row 3: Ch 2, turn, bphdc around next 2 sts, * fphdc around next 3 sts, bphdc around next 2 sts, rep from * to last st, hdc in last st (69 hdc).

Row 4: Ch 3, fpdc in next 2 sts, sk next st, hdc in next 2 sts, dc in prev sk st, * sk next st, hdc in next 2 sts, dc in prev sk st, rep from * to last 3 sts, fpdc in next 2 sts, dc in 1st ch of last st (69 sts).

Row 5: Ch 2, turn, bpdc in next 2 sts, hdc in next st and in each st across to last 3 sts, bpdc in next 2 sts, hdc in last st (69 sts).

Rows 6–31: Rep Rows 4 and 5.

Note: *You can make the leg warmers as wide or as narrow as you like by adjusting Rows 6–31. My pattern has a 13" (33cm) circumference. Rows 4 and 5 measure 1" (2.5cm) across, so you can adjust the size to your liking.*

Row 32: Ch 2, turn, fphdc around next 2 sts, * bphdc around next 3 sts, fphdc around next 2 sts, rep from * to last st, hdc in last st (69 hdc).

Row 33: Ch 2, turn, bphdc around next 2 sts, * fphdc around next 3 sts, bphdc around next 2 sts, rep from * to last st, hdc in last st (69 hdc).

Fasten off. Weave in ends.

Frilled Edging

With RS of leg warmer facing

With H hook and TC, join yarn in any st around leg warmer.

Rnd 1: Ch 1, sc in same st as joining, sc evenly around the leg warmer working 3 sc in each corner st, making sure there is an even number of sc around; join with sl st in beg sc.

Rnd 2: (Ch 2, sl st) in same st as joining, sl st in next st, * (sl st, ch 2, sl st) in next st, sl st in next st, rep from * around; join with sl st in joining sl st from Rnd 1.

Fasten off. Weave in ends.

Finishing Touches

To complete your leg warmers, sew 1 button in between Rows 1 and 2 in the middle of each 2 post ridges (14 buttons/leg warmer). To fasten, button into the middle ridges of the opposite side of leg warmers. Make 2 motifs of your choice from Chapter 3 and attach them to any button on the leg warmers. The motifs can be changed to match any color in your wardrobe.

Large Market Bag

BEGINNER

This bag is big, soft and holds so much! There are two handle sizes, one for holding with your hand, and one to wear over your shoulder. It also has a rectangular bottom, which means more room for your groceries. Since it's made from worsted weight cotton yarn, it's eco-friendly, too, and will last for several years. This would also make the perfect bag for your crochet projects, or a fabulous beach bag, too. Don't forget to finish it off with some cute flower motifs!

MATERIALS

Worsted weight cotton yarn **4**
in 2 colors of your choice:

Color 1: 200 yds (183m)

Color 2: 175 yds (160m)

Size I (5.5mm) crochet hook

⅞"–1" (2.2cm–2.5cm) buttons
(one per motif)

Scissors

Tapestry needle

Finished Project Sizes

32" circumference × 12½" high
(81.5cm × 31.8cm), not including
handles

Gauge

No gauge required

Glossary of Abbreviations

beg	beginning
bphdc	back post half double crochet
ch(s)	chain(s)
dc	double crochet
hdc	half double crochet
rep	repeat
rnd(s)	round(s)
sc	single crochet
sk	skip
sl st	slip stitch
sp(s)	space(s)
st(s)	stitch(es)
*	repeat instructions following the asterisk as directed
C1	color 1
C2	color 2

Market Bag

To create the base, ch 40 with C1.

Row 1: Hdc in 3rd ch from hook and in each st across (39 hdc).

Rows 2–11: Ch 2, turn, hdc in next st and in each st across (39 hdc).

Do not fasten off.

Rnd 1: (Working around 4 sides) Ch 2, turn, bphdc in next 37 sts, hdc in corner st, work 11 hdc evenly along side, hdc in corner st, bphdc in next 37 sts, hdc in corner st, work 11 hdc evenly along last side; join with sl st in 2nd ch of beg ch-2 (100 hdc).

Rnd 2: Ch 2, hdc in next st and in each st around; join C2 with sl st in 2nd ch of beg ch-2 (100 hdc).

Rnd 3: Ch 2, hdc in next st, dc in next 3 sts, hdc in next 2 sts, sc in next 3 sts, * hdc in next 2 sts, dc in next 3 sts, hdc in next 2 sts, sc in next 3 sts, rep from * around; join with sl st in 2nd ch of beg ch-2 (100 sts).

Rnd 4: Ch 2, hdc in next st, dc in next 3 sts, hdc in next 2 sts, sc in next 3 sts, * hdc in next 2 sts, dc in next 3 sts, hdc in next 2 sts, sc in next 3 sts, rep from * around; join C1 with sl st in 2nd ch of beg ch-2 (100 sts).

Rnd 5: Ch 2, hdc in next st and in each st around; join C2 with sl st in 2nd ch of beg ch-2 (100 hdc).

Rnd 6: Ch 2, hdc in next st, sc in next 3 sts, hdc in next 2 sts, dc in next 3 sts, * hdc in next 2 sts, sc in next 3 sts, hdc in next 2 sts, dc in next 3 sts, rep from * around; join with sl st in 2nd ch of beg ch-2 (100 sts).

Rnd 7: Ch 2, hdc in next st, sc in next 3 sts, hdc in next 2 sts, dc in next 3 sts, * hdc in next 2 sts, sc in next 3 sts, hdc in next 2 sts, dc in next 3 sts, rep from * around; join C1 with sl st in 2nd ch of beg ch-2 (100 sts).

Rnd 8: Ch 2, hdc in next st and in each st around; join C2 with sl st in 2nd ch of beg ch-2 (100 hdc).

Rnds 9–28: Rep Rnds 3–8, ending on Rnd 4.

Rnd 29: Ch 1, sc in same st as joining and in each st around; join with sl st in beg sc (100 sc).

Rnd 30: Ch 1, sc in same st as joining and in next 25 sts, ch 26, sk next 15 sts, sc in next 37 sts, ch 26, sk next 15, sc in last 7 sts; join with sl st in beg sc (70 sc, 52 chs).

Rnd 31: Ch 1, sc in same st as joining and in next 25 sc, hdc in next 26 ch, sc in next 37 sc, hdc in next 26 ch, sc in last 7 sc; join with sl st in beg sc (70 sc, 52 hdc).

Rnd 32: Ch 1, sc in same st as joining and in next 25 sc, hdc in next 26 hdc, sc in next 37 sc, hdc in next 26 hdc, sc in last 7 sc; join with sl st in beg sc (70 sc, 52 hdc).

Rnd 33: Ch 1, sc in same st as joining and in next 25 sc, ch 76, sk next 26 hdc, sc in next 37 sc, ch 76, sk next 26 hdc, sc in last 7 sc; join with sl st in beg sc (70 sc, 152 chs).

Rnd 34: Ch 1, sc in same st as joining and in next 25 sc, hdc in next 76 ch, sc in next 37 sc, hdc in next 76 ch, sc in last 7 sc; join with sl st in beg sc (70 sc, 152 hdc).

Rnd 35: Ch 1, sc in same st as joining and in next 25 sc, hdc in next 76 hdc, sc in next 37 sc, hdc in next 76 hdc, sc in last 7 sc; join with sl st in beg sc (70 sc, 152 hdc).

Rnd 36: Ch 1, sl st in same st as joining and in each st around; join with sl st in beg ch-1 (222 sl sts).

Fasten off. Weave in ends.

Finishing Touches

To complete your market bag, make motifs of your choice from Chapter 3 and sew buttons onto the front or back of the bag. Button the motifs onto the bag. If you would like to use the motifs as a permanent addition to your bag, you may sew parts of the motifs onto the bag. They can be easily removed and replaced with new ones whenever you would like a change.

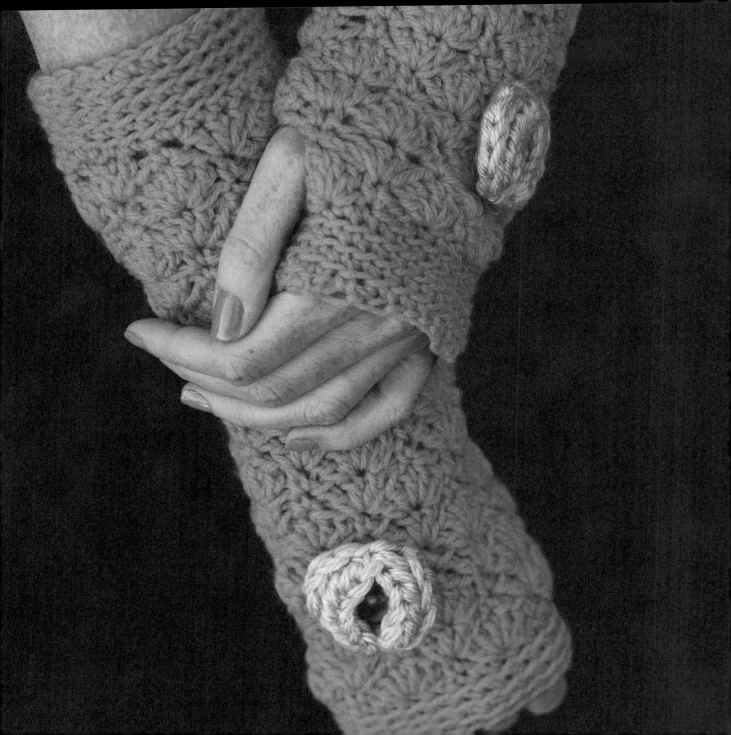

Scalloped Fingerless Gloves

The tight stitch of these gloves will keep your arms warm and your fingers free. By making several motifs in different colors, you can interchange them to match all of your outfits. Whether you make the long or short version of this warmer, these fingerless gloves will become your new favorite accessory! Wear them with long sleeves to stay extra comfy.

MATERIALS

Sport weight yarn **(3)** in the color of your choice

Arm length: 130 yds (119m)

Wrist length: 90 yds (83m)

Size I (5.5mm) crochet hook

Two ⅞"–1" (2.2cm–2.5cm) buttons

Scissors

Stitch markers

Tapestry needle

Finished Project Sizes

Arm warmers: 8" circumference × 11½" long (20.5cm × 29.2cm)

Wrist warmers: 8" circumference × 7" long (20.5cm × 17.8cm)

Gauge

15 sts = 4" (10.2cm)

7 rows dc = 4" (10.2cm)

Glossary of Abbreviations

beg	beginning
blp	back loop
ch(s)	chain(s)
dc	double crochet
prev	previous
rep	repeat
rnd(s)	round(s)
sc	single crochet
sk	skip
sl st	slip stitch
st(s)	stitch(es)
*	repeat instructions following the asterisk as directed

Scalloped Fingerless Gloves (make 2)

Bottom Cuff

Ch 25, being careful not to twist the ch; join with sl st in beg ch.

Rnd 1: Ch 1, sc in same st as joining and in each ch around (25 sc).

Continue working *Bottom Cuff* in rounds, placing a st marker in the beg sc.

Rnds 2–5: * Sc in blp of next st and in blp of each st around, rep from * around (25 sc).

Middle

Working through both loops:

Rnd 6: Join with sl st in beg st marker sc, then remove st marker, ch 1, sc in same st as joining, * sk next st, work 5 dc in next st (scallop made), sk next st, sc in next sc, rep from * around to last 4 sts, sk next st, work 5 dc in next st, sk next 2 sts; join with sl st in beg sc (6 scallops).

Rnd 7: Do not ch, sl st in next 2 dc, (sl st, ch 1, sc) in next dc, ch 5 (thumb hole), sk next 5 sts, sc in next st, sk next 2 sts, work 3 dc in sc (between the next 2 scallops from prev rnd), * sk next 2 sts, sc in next st, sk next 2 sts, work 3 dc in sc (between the next 2 scallops from prev rnd), rep from * around; join with sl st in beg sc (6 sc,15 dc).

Rnd 8: Ch 1, sc in same st as joining, sk next 2 ch, work 5 dc in next ch, sk next 2 ch, sc in next sc, * sk next st, work 5 dc in next st, sk next st, sc in next sc, rep from * around to last 3 sts, sk next st, work 5 dc in next st, sk next st; join with sl st in beg sc (6 scallops).

Rnd 9: Do not ch, sl st in next 2 dc, (sl st, ch 1, sc) in next dc, * sk next 2 sts, work 3 dc in sc (between the next 2 scallops from prev rnd), sk next 2 sts, sc in next st, rep from * around; join with sl st in beg sc (6 sc, 18 dc).

Rnd 10: Ch 1, sc in same st as joining, * sk next st, work 5 dc in next st, sk next st, sc in next sc, rep from * around to last 3 sts; sk next st, work 5 dc in next st, sk last st; join with sl st in beg sc (6 scallops).

Do not fasten off. Continue with desired style below.

For Wrist Warmers

Rnds 11–15: Rep Rnds 9 and 10, ending on Rnd 9.

Do not fasten off. Continue with *Top Cuff for Wrist Warmers* below.

Top Cuff for Wrist Warmers

Rnd 1: Ch 1, 2 sc in same st as joining, sc in next st and in each st around (25 sc).

Continue working in rounds, placing a st marker in the beg sc.

Rnds 2–4: * Sc in blp of next st and in blp of each st around, rep from * around (25 sc).

Rnd 5: * Sc in blp of next st and in blp of each st around, rep from * around, sl st through blp of next st, sl st through both loops of next st (25 sc, 2 sl sts).

Fasten off and weave in ends.

For Arm Warmers

Continue below with Rnd 11.

Rnds 11–25: Rep Rnds 9 and 10, ending on Rnd 9.

Do not fasten off. Continue with *Top Cuff for Arm Warmers* below.

Top Cuff for Arm Warmers

Rnd 1: Ch 1, 2 sc in same st as joining, * sc in next 3 sts, 2 sc in next st, rep from * around to last 3 sts, sc in next 2 sts, 2 sc in last st (31 sc).

Continue working in rnds, placing a st marker in the beg sc.

Rnds 2–4: * Sc in blp of next st and in blp of each st around, rep from * around (31 sc).

Rnd 5: * Sc in blp of next st and in blp of each st around, rep from * around, sl st through blp of next st, sl st through both loops of next st (31 sc, 2 sl st).

Fasten off and weave in ends.

Finishing Touches

Choose your favorite motifs from Chapter 3 and sew buttons onto the gloves where you would like the motifs placed. Button the motifs onto the buttons. Make new motifs and switch them out when you want to change your look.

Wavy Cowl

Prepare yourself for lots of compliments when you're wearing this cozy cowl. The wave pattern gives it a fresh, unique and fashionable look. Try using a bulky yarn and a bigger hook to make it extra luxurious. This is a great pattern for beginners, and since they work up in no time, they make great last-minute gifts!

MATERIALS

Worsted weight yarn (4) in the color of your choice: 300 yds–400 yds (275m–366m), depending on the thickness of the yarn

Size L (8mm) crochet hook

⅞"–1" (2.2cm–2.5cm) button

Scissors

Tapestry needle

Finished Project Sizes

One size: 30"–33" circumference × 20" long (76.2–83.8cm × 50.8cm)

Gauge

No gauge required.

Glossary of Abbreviations

beg	beginning
bptr	back post treble crochet
ch(s)	chain(s)
hdc	half double crochet
rep	repeat
rnd(s)	round(s)
sk	skip
sl st	slip stitch
st(s)	stitch(es)
tr	treble crochet
*	repeat instructions following the asterisk as directed
( )	work instructions within parentheses as many times as directed

Wavy Cowl

Ch 68, being careful not to twist the ch; join with sl st in beg ch.

Rnd 1: Ch 4, tr in same st as joining, (2 tr in next ch) 5 times, (sk next ch, tr) 5 times, sk next ch, * (2 tr in next ch) 6 times, (sk next ch, tr) 5 times, sk next ch, rep from * around; join with sl st in 4th ch of beg ch-4 (68 tr).

Rnd 2: Ch 4, bptr in next st and in each st around; join with sl st in 4th ch of beg ch-4 (68 tr).

Rnds 3–18: Rep Rnds 1 and 2.

Rnd 19: Ch 2, hdc in next st and in each st around; join with sl st in 2nd ch of beg ch-2 (68 hdc).

Fasten off. Sew in ends.

Chapter 3
Interchangeable Flowers & Motifs

It's true, I'm a tad obsessed with interchangeable motifs. I'm always thinking of the next one I want to create and envisioning them on my designs. Not only can all of the flowers and motifs interchange on all of the projects in this book, but you can also mix-and-match them with all the hats and hair treasures in my first book, *Blooming Crochet Hats*. There are so many options to choose from, it will be hard to pick just one!

Don't feel obligated to use the yarns I chose to make the flowers and motifs. You can create them in plenty of other ways by using different textures and thicknesses of yarns, and by using different hook sizes, too. Every one you create will be a true masterpiece!

Kitty Cat

These kitty motifs are just "purr"fect! Why not make some cute hair accessories out of these? Make them up in lots of colors to match your little one's wardrobe, then attach them to hair clips or headbands. While you're at it, make some matching ones. Then the next time she plays dress-up with her doll, they can wear the same hair accents!

MATERIALS

Small amount of sport weight yarn **3** in the color of your choice

Small amount of sport weight yarn **3** for eyes, whiskers and mouth

Size H (5mm) crochet hook

Scissors

Tapestry needle

Finished Project Size

3" × 2½" (7.6cm × 6.4cm)

Gauge

No gauge required.

 See **Stitches & Techniques** for instructions on the 3 double crochet cluster stitch (3dc-cl).

Glossary of Abbreviations

3dc-cl	double crochet cluster
beg	beginning
ch(s)	chain(s)
dc	double crochet
hdc	half double crochet
rnd(s)	round(s)
sc	single crochet
sl st	slip stitch
st(s)	stitch(es)
( )	work instructions within parentheses as many times as directed

Make the Kitty Cat

Ch 5; join with sl st in beg ch to form ring.

Rnd 1: Ch 3, work 3 dc, 3 hdc, 4 dc, 3 hdc in ring; join with sl st in 3rd ch of beg ch-3 (14 sts).

Rnd 2: Ch 2, hdc in same st as joining, 2 hdc in next 3 sts, 2 sc in next 3 sts, 2 hdc in next 4 sts, 2 sc in last 3 sts; join with sl st in 2nd ch of beg ch-2 (28 sts).

Rnd 3: Ch 1, sc in same st as joining and in next 5 sts, sl st in next st, (sc, 3dc-cl) in next st, (hdc, ch 1, sl st) in next st, sl st in next 5 sts, (sl st, hdc) in next st, (3dc-cl, ch 1, sc) in next st, sl st in next st, sc in next 7 sts, sl st in last 4 sts; join with sl st in beg ch-1.

Fasten off. Weave in ends.

Finishing Touches

Using sport weight yarn in the color of your choice, sew eyes and a mouth onto the motif (use the project photos as a guide).

Next, cut a piece of sport weight yarn for the whiskers. Untwist the yarn to separate the strands. Using one strand, thread a needle and sew the whiskers onto the cheeks (use the project photos as a guide).

Fasten off. Weave in ends.

Darling Daffodil

These darling flowers would be perfect for decorating a kitchen. Sew some of those special vintage buttons you've been saving up onto your kitchen curtains to create a fabulous trim, or add some to the corners of your placemats. The possibilities are endless!

MATERIALS

Small amount of sport weight yarn **(3)** in 2 colors of your choice

Size I (5.5mm) crochet hook

Tapestry needle

Scissors

Finished Project Size

3½" (8.9cm)

Gauge

No gauge required.

Glossary of Abbreviations

beg	beginning
blp	back loop
ch(s)	chain(s)
dc	double crochet
flp	front loop
hdc	half double crochet
sc	single crochet
sl st	slip stitch
st(s)	stitch(es)
rep	repeat
rnd	round
*	repeat instructions following the asterisk as directed
( )	work instructions within parentheses as many times as directed
MC	main color
TC	trim color

Make the Darling Daffodil

With MC, ch 5; join with sl st in beg ch to form ring.

Rnd 1: Ch 1, work 12 sc in ring; join with sl st in flp of beg sc (12 sc).

Rnd 2: Ch 1, sc in the flp of joining st and in each flp st around; join with sl st in beg sc (12 sc).

Fasten off. Weave in ends.

Join TC with sl st in any unworked blp st behind Rnd 2.

Rnd 3: Ch 1, (sl st, ch 4, sc in 2nd ch from hook, hdc in next ch, dc in last ch) in next blp, sl st in next blp, * (sl st, ch 4, sc in 2nd ch from hook, hdc in next ch, dc in last ch) in next blp, sl st in next blp, rep from * around; join with sl st in beg ch-1 (6 petals made).

Fasten off. Weave in ends.

Puppy Dog

Looking for that one-of-a-kind baby shower gift? Why not make a pair of slippers and attach these cute puppy motifs to them? These puppies are easy to whip up in any color. By adding the same motifs to a handmade baby outfit, you can create a gorgeous layette set!

MATERIALS

Small amount of sport weight yarn in 2 colors of your choice

Small amount of black sport weight yarn

Size H (5mm) crochet hook

Tapestry needle

Scissors

Finished Project Size

3½" × 2½ (8.9cm × 6.4cm)

Gauge

No gauge required.

Glossary of Abbreviations

beg	beginning
ch(s)	chain(s)
dc	double crochet
hdc	half double crochet
rnd	round
sc	single crochet
sl st	slip stitch
st(s)	stitch(es)
yo	yarn over
( )	work instructions within parentheses as many times as directed
MC	main color
TC	trim color

Make the Puppy Dog

With MC, ch 5; join with sl st in beg ch to form ring.

Rnd 1: Ch 2, work 13 hdc in ring; join with sl st in 2nd ch of beg ch-2 (14 hdc).

Rnd 2: Ch 1, sc in same st as joining, (hdc, dc) in next st, 2 dc in next st, (dc, hdc) in next st, sc in next st, (hdc, 2 dc) in next st, (dc, hdc) in next st, sc in next 3 sts, (hdc, dc) in next st, (2 dc, hdc) in next st, sc in last 2 sts; join with sl st in beg sc (23 sts).

Rnd 3: Ch 1, sl st in next st, ch 5, (hdc, dc) in 2nd ch from hook, 3 dc in next ch, (dc, hdc) in next ch, 2 hdc in last ch, sl st in next 3 sts, ch 10, 3 dc in 3rd ch from hook, (yo, insert hook in next ch, draw up loop) 3 times, yo and draw through 7 loops on hook, (yo, insert hook in next ch, draw up loop) 2 times, yo and draw through 5 loops on hook, (yo, insert hook in next ch, draw up loop) 2 times, yo and draw through 5 loops on hook, sl st in next st.

Fasten off. Weave in ends.

Eye Patch

With TC, ch 2.

Rnd 1: Work 7 sc in 1st ch st; join with sl st in beg sc (7 sc).

Pull beginning tail tight to close the hole. Leaving a long end for sewing, fasten off. Sew the eye patch onto the motif and weave in ends.

Facial Features

With a small amount of black sport weight yarn, sew the eyes and mouth onto the motif (use project photos as a guide).

Hoot the Owl

"Whoo" doesn't love owls? Envision a little boy curled up in his newly crocheted blanket, or a little girl proudly wearing her new hair treasure, both trimmed with these adorable owl motifs. You could also use a few of these owls to trim the masterpiece drawing that your little artist made you, then frame it for everyone to see.

MATERIALS

Owl body: Small amount of worsted weight yarn in 3 colors of your choice

Eyes: Small amount of white and black sport weight yarn

Beak: Small amount of orange sport weight yarn

Size H (5mm) crochet hook

Size I (5.5mm) crochet hook

Scissors

Tapestry needle

Finished Project Size

2¾" × 3" (7.6cm × 6.7cm)

Gauge

No gauge required.

> Want more options? Try using buttons or googly eyes for the eyes, or felt for the beak.
>
> For instructions on the picot stitch, see **Stitches & Techniques**.

Glossary of Abbreviations

beg	beginning
ch(s)	chain(s)
dc	double crochet
hdc	half double crochet
rnd	round
sc	single crochet
sl st	slip stitch
st(s)	stitch(es)
( )	work instructions within parentheses as many times as directed
C1	color 1
C2	color 2
C3	color 3

Make Hoot the Owl

With I hook and C1, ch 5; join with sl st in beg ch to form ring.

Rnd 1: Ch 1, work 12 sc in ring; join C2 with sl st in beg sc (12 sc).

Rnd 2: Ch 1, 2 sc in same st as joining and in each st around; join C3 with sl st in beg sc (24 sc).

Rnd 3: Ch 1, sc in same st as joining and in each st around; join with sl st in beg sc (24 sc).

Rnd 4: Ch 1, (sl st, ch 2, dc, ch 3, picot st, hdc) in next st, sc in next 3 sc, (hdc, dc, ch 3, picot st, hdc) in next st, sl st in next 19 sts; join with sl st in beg ch-1 st.

Fasten off. Weave in ends.

Finishing Touches

Beak

With H hook and orange yarn:

Row 1: Ch 2, work 2 sc in 1st ch st (2 sc).

Row 2: Ch 1, turn, 2 sc in next 2 sts (4 sc).

Weave beginning yarn end in.

Leave enough yarn at the end to sew the beak onto the owl, then fasten off. Next, thread the tapestry needle with the orange yarn end and sew the beak onto the motif (use project photos as a guide).

Eyes (make 2)

With H hook and white yarn:

Rnd 1: Ch 2, work 8 sc in 1st ch, join with sl st in beg sc (8 sc).

Rnd 2: Do not ch, sl st in next st and in next 6 sts, join with sl st in beg sl st (7 sl sts).

Leave a long end for sewing and fasten off. Pull the beginning tail tight to close the hole, weave in and trim.

Pupils (make 2)

With H hook and black yarn:

Rnd 1: Ch 2, (sc, sl st) in 1st ch, (1 sc, 1 sl st).

Leave a long end for sewing and fasten off. Pull the beginning tail tight to close the hole, then cut the end short.

Putting the Eyes Together

Thread the tapestry needle with the long black tail, place the black pupil on the center of the white eye with the short end tucked behind and sew into place. Next, thread the tapestry needle with the white yarn end and sew both eyes onto the motif above the beak.

Little Monster

These monsters are far from scary! They'll make great additions to handmade party invitations or thank-you notes. Just sew a button onto the card and attach them—simple and easy. Upcycle the motif by handing out party favors with buttons, so your guests can move the motif from their invitations to a new item they'll enjoy!

MATERIALS

Small amount of sport weight yarn  in 2 colors of your choice

Small amount of black sport weight yarn

Size H (5mm) crochet hook

Scissors

Tapestry needle

Finished Project Size

2½" × 3½" (6.4cm × 8.9cm)

Gauge

No gauge required.

Glossary of Abbreviations

beg	beginning
ch(s)	chain(s)
dc	double crochet
hdc	half double crochet
rep	repeat
rnd	round
sc	single crochet
sl st	slip stitch
st(s)	stitch(es)
tr	treble crochet
yo	yarn over
()	work instructions within parentheses as many times as directed
MC	main color (body)
EC	eye color
BC	border color (eye trim)

Make the Little Monster

With EC, ch 5; join with sl st in beg ch to form ring.

Rnd 1: Ch 2 (counts as hdc), work 13 hdc in ring; join MC with sl st in 2nd ch of beg ch-2 (14 hdc).

Rnd 2: Ch 1, sl st in same st as joining, (sl st, ch 2, sl st in 2nd ch from hook, sl st, ch 3, sc in 2nd ch from hook, sl st in last ch, sl st, ch 2, sl st in 2nd ch from hook, sl st) in next st, sc in next st, hdc in next st, 2 hdc in next st, (2 dc, tr) in next st, 3 tr in next st, (dc, ch 4, sk next ch, 3 hdc in next ch, sl st in last 2 chs, picot st, dc, ch 5, 3 hdc in 2nd ch from hook, sk next 2 chs, sl st in last ch, picot st) in next st, 3 tr in next st, (tr, 2 dc) in next st, 2 hdc in next st, hdc in next 2 sts, sc in last st; join with sl st in beg ch-1.

Fasten off. Weave in ends.

Finishing Touches

Using a small amount of black sport weight yarn, thread your tapestry needle and sew a mouth onto your LITTLE MONSTER (use the project photos as a guide for placement).

Adding the Border Trim to Eyes

After creating your LITTLE MONSTER, follow the steps below:

1. Using C3, insert the hook through any st between Rnds 1 and 2.

2. Draw the BC yarn up through the st.

3. Insert the hook into the next st, yo and sl st; continue around to the last st.

4. When you get to the last st, drop the loop off your hook and place the hook underneath the motif; insert the hook from the bottom up into the center of the 1st sl st made. With your fingers, place the loop over the hook and draw it down through the center of the 1st sl st.

5. Cut the yarn and pull the end through the loop. Pull tight, tie both ends together and weave in ends.

 See **Stitches & Techniques** for picot stitch and slip stitch border illustrations.

Loopy Flower

The delicate petals on this flower will definitely provide a soft feel to any item. Add these dainty flowers to a handmade scarf and hat set or use a thicker yarn to create a trendy brooch or a beautiful bow for a special gift.

MATERIALS

Small amount of sport weight yarn **(3)** in 2 colors of your choice

Size I (5.5mm) crochet hook

Scissors

Tapestry needle

Glossary of Abbreviations

beg	beginning
blp(s)	back loops
bp	back post
bpsc	back post single crochet
ch(s)	chain(s)
flp(s)	front loops
fpsc	front post single crochet
hdc	half double crochet
rep	repeat
rnd	round
sc	single crochet
sl st	slip stitch
st(s)	stitch(es)
( )	work instructions within parentheses as many times as directed

Finished Project Size

3½" (8.9cm)

Gauge

No gauge required.

Make the Regular Loopy Flower

Note: *The petals of the REGULAR LOOPY FLOWER are worked in the front posts and back posts.*

Ch 5; join with sl st in beg ch to form ring.

Rnd 1: Ch 2 (counts as hdc), work 13 hdc in ring; join with sl st in 2nd ch of beg ch-2 (14 hdc).

Rnd 2: Ch 1, bpsc around same st as joining, ch 10, fpsc around next st, ch 10, (bpsc around next st, ch 10, fpsc around next st, ch 10) 6 times; join with bp sl st around the beg post (14 ch loops).

Fasten off. Weave in ends.

Make the Puffy Loopy Flower

Note: *The petals of the PUFFY LOOPY FLOWER are worked in the front loops and back loops.*

Ch 5, join with sl st in beg ch to form ring.

Rnd 1: Ch 3 (counts as hdc), work 13 hdc in ring, join with sl st in 2nd ch of beg ch-2 (14 hdc).

Rnd 2: Do not ch, (flp sc in next st, ch 10, blp sc in next st, ch 10) 7 times; join with fp sl st around the beg flp sc (14 ch loops).

Rnd 3: Ch 10, (blp sc in next unworked blp, ch 10, flp sc in next unworked flp, ch 10) 7 times; join with sl st in beg blp sc (28 ch loops).

Fasten off. Weave in ends.

Pretty Petunia

There are so many ways to create with this PRETTY PETUNIA. Just let your imagination run wild! Add them to a crocheted belt and interchange them to match your outfit, or use scrap pieces of cotton yarn and whip up a few bath wipes for babies or face scrubbies. Sew two together, back to back, and use them as scrub pads to wash dishes.

MATERIALS

Small amount of sport weight yarn in 3 colors of your choice

Size I (5.5mm) crochet hook

Scissors

Tapestry needle

Finished Project Size

3¼" (8.3cm)

Gauge

No gauge required.

Glossary of Abbreviations

ch(s)	chain(s)
st(s)	stitch(es)
sl st	slip stitch
beg	beginning
sk	skip
rep	repeat
rnd	round
sc	single crochet
dc	double crochet
( )	work instructions within the parentheses as many times as directed
C1	color 1
C2	color 2
C3	color 3

Make the Pretty Petunia

With C1, ch 5; join with sl st in beg ch to form ring.

Rnd 1: Ch 1, work 12 sc in ring; join C2 with sl st in beg sc (12 sc).

Rnd 2: Ch 1, 2 sc in same st as joining, * 2 sc in next st, rep from * around; join C3 with sl st in beg sc (24 sc).

Rnd 3: Do not ch, sl st in same st as joining, sk next st, 7 dc in next st, sk next st, sl st in next st, (sk next 2 sts, 7 dc in next st, sk next st, sl st in next st) 3 times, sk next 2 sts, 7 dc in next st, sk last st, join with sl st in beg sl st (5 petals).

Fasten off. Weave in ends.

Out of This World Rocket

These rocket motifs truly are out of this world! Make them as colorful or as simple as you like. Use them to decorate a scrapbook or to trim an afghan for your child's room. Make them out of cotton yarn and use them as tub toys.

MATERIALS

Small amount of sport weight yarn in 3 colors of your choice

Small amount of black sport weight yarn

Size I (5.5mm) crochet hook

Scissors

Tapestry needle

Finished Project Size

3½" × 3½" (8.9cm × 8.9cm)

Gauge

No gauge required.

Glossary of Abbreviations

beg	beginning
ch(s)	chain(s)
dc	double crochet
hdc	half double crochet
rep	repeat
rnd	round
sc	single crochet
sk	skip
sl st	slip stitch
st(s)	stitch(es)
tr	treble crochet
()	work instructions within parentheses as many times as directed
MC	main color
TC	trim color
BC	border color

Make the Rocket

With MC, ch 5; join with sl st in beg ch to form ring.

Rnd 1: Ch 1, work 14 sc in ring, join with sl st in beg sc (14 sc).

Rnd 2: Ch 1, (sc, hdc, dc) in same st as joining, dc in next 2 sts, (dc, hdc, sc) in next st, sc in next 3 sts, (sc, hdc, dc) in next st, dc in next 2 sts, (dc, hdc, sc) in next st, sc in last 3 sts; join with sl st in beg sc (22 sts).

Rnd 3: Do not ch, (sl st, ch 1, sc) in next st, sc in next 3 sts, (sc, sl st) in next st, sl st in next st; join TC with sl st in next st, (ch 4, tr, dc) in same st as joining, dc in next st, (hdc, sc) in next st, sc in next st, sl st in next 2 sts, sk next st, (3 dc, tr) in next st, (tr, 3 dc) in next st, sk next st, sl st in next 2 sts, sc in next st, hdc in next st, dc in next st, (dc, tr, ch 4, sl st) in next st.

Fasten off. Weave in ends.

Adding the Border

After creating your rocket, follow the steps below:

1. Using BC, insert hook through any st in the last rnd of MC.

2. Draw the yarn up through the st.

3. Insert the hook into the next st and sl st around the outside of entire shape, making sure to work 2 sl sts in each of the 4 corner sts; continue to the last st.

4. When you get to the last st, drop the loop off your hook and place the hook underneath the rocket; insert the hook from the bottom up into the center of the 1st sl st made. With your fingers, place the loop over the hook and draw it down through the center of the 1st sl st.

5. Cut the yarn and pull the end through the loop. Pull tight, tie both ends together and weave in ends.

 See **Stitches & Techniques** for slip stitch border illustrations.

Sweet Rosebud

These tiny rosebuds will put a smile on anyone's face. Mix and match them on your arm warmers or boot cuffs for an elegant look. They would also be cute attached to a bracelet or a choker. These rosebuds will add a big punch to any project!

MATERIALS

Small amount of worsted weight yarn (4) or 2 strands of sport weight yarn (3) in the color of your choice

Size I (5.5mm) crochet hook

Scissors

Tapestry needle

Finished Project Size

1¾" (4.4cm)

Gauge

No gauge required.

Glossary of Abbreviations

beg	beginning
blp(s)	back loop(s)
ch(s)	chain(s)
flp(s)	front loop(s)
hdc	half double crochet
prev	previous
rep	repeat
rnd	round
sc	single crochet
sl st	slip stitch
st(s)	stitch(es)

Make the Sweet Rosebud

Ch 5; join with sl st in beg ch to form ring.

Rnd 1: Ch 1, work 12 sc in ring; join with sl st in flp of beg sc (12 sc).

Rnd 2: Do not ch, hdc in same flp st as joining and in flp of next 5 sts, then hdc in blp of next 6 sts (12 hdc).

Rnd 3: Do not join, hdc in the 6 prev unworked blps of Rnd 2, then hdc in the 6 prev unworked flps of Rnd 2, insert hook in next ch st (directly after hdc just made) and in st directly behind it, sl st (12 hdc).

Fasten off. Weave in ends.

Spiral Flower

A simple twist of petals provides a fun and interesting look on this SPIRAL FLOWER. When the regular size is complete, the petals stand up, making the flower look like a pinwheel. With the larger size, the petals lay down, giving the flower a tidy look. Use these to embellish clothes or purses or to give your home décor a more personal touch by adding a few to your lamp shades or pillows.

MATERIALS

Small amount of worsted weight yarn  or 2 strands of sport weight yarn in color of your choice

Size I (5.5mm) crochet hook

Scissors

Tapestry needle

Finished Project Size

Regular: 3¼" (8.3cm)

Large: 3½" (8.9cm)

Gauge

No gauge required.

Glossary of Abbreviations

beg	beginning
ch(s)	chain(s)
hdc	half double crochet
rep	repeat
rnd	round
RS	right side
sc	single crochet
sl st	slip stitch
sp(s)	space(s)
st(s)	stitch(es)
()	work instructions within parentheses as many times as directed

Make the Regular Spiral Flower

Ch 5; join with sl st in beg ch to form ring.

Rnd 1: Ch 1, work 11 sc in ring; join with sl st in beg sc (11 sc).

Rnd 2: (Ch 5, sl st in next st, turn, work 9 hdc in ch sp just made; holding petal and hook stationary, turn the center ring of flower to the right so the RS of the ring is facing, insert hook in next unworked sc, sl st) 5 times, ch 5, sl st in next st, turn, work 9 hdc in ch sp just made; holding petal and hook stationary, turn the center ring of flower to the right so the RS of the ring is facing; join with sl st in beg sl st (6 petals made).

Fasten off. Weave in ends.

Make the Large Spiral Flower

Ch 5; join with sl st in beg ch to form ring.

Rnd 1: Ch 1, work 11 sc in ring; join with sl st in beg sc (11 sc).

Rnd 2: (Ch 7, sl st in next st, turn, work 12 hdc in ch sp just made; holding petal and hook stationary, turn the center ring of flower to the right so the RS of ring is facing, insert hook in next unworked sc, sl st) 5 times, ch 7, sl st in next st, turn, work 12 hdc in ch sp just made; holding petal and hook stationary, turn the center ring of flower to the right so the RS of ring is facing; join with sl st in beg sl st (6 petals made).

Fasten off. Weave in ends.

Ladybug

This LADYBUG is too cute for words! These motifs will be adorable buttoned on your little one's sunhat or added as a border to your crocheted picnic blanket. This is definitely a great motif to whip up for spring and summer!

MATERIALS

Small amount of sport weight yarn in 2 colors of your choice

Small amount of black sport weight yarn

Size H (5mm) crochet hook

Scissors

Tapestry needle

Finished Project Size

2¾" (7cm)

Gauge

No gauge required.

Glossary of Abbreviations

beg	beginning
ch(s)	chain(s)
hdc	half double crochet
rep	repeat
rnd	round
RS	right side
sc	single crochet
sl st	slip stitch
st(s)	stitch(es)
WS	wrong side
*	repeat instructions following the asterisk as directed
MC	main color
TC	trim color

Make the Ladybug

With MC, ch 5; join with sl st in beg ch to form ring.

Rnd 1: Ch 2 (counts as hdc), work 11 hdc in ring; join TC with sl st in 2nd ch of beg ch-2 (12 hdc).

Rnd 2: Ch 2, hdc in same st as joining, * 2 hdc in next st, rep from * around; join with sl st in 2nd ch of beg ch-2 (24 hdc).

Rnd 3: Ch 1, sc in same st as joining, 2 sc in next st, * sc in next st, 2 sc in next st, rep from * around; join with sl st in beg sc (36 sc).

Fasten off. Weave in ends.

Finishing Touches

Head

With RS of the LADYBUG facing you, insert hook in last sc made and join TC.

Row 1: (Ch 1, hdc) in same st as joining, 2 hdc in next st, (hdc, ch 1, sl st) in next st.

Fasten off. Weave in ends.

Line to Separate Wings

Using TC, thread your tapestry needle and insert needle up from the bottom of the motif through the middle base st of the head (see project photos for placement), then insert needle close to the button hole, making sure to form a straight line.

Fasten off. Weave in ends.

Next, insert the tapestry needle up from the bottom of the motif on the opposite side of the button hole (directly across from the top line), then insert it down through the bottom sc to form a straight line (see project photo for placement), making sure the bottom line is aligned with the top line.

Fasten off. Weave in ends.

Spots (make 4)

With TC, ch 2.

Rnd 1: Work 5 sc in 1st ch; join with sl st in beg sc (5 sc).

Leaving an 8"–10" (20.3cm–25.4cm) tail, fasten off and weave in beginning end (do not sew in tail just made).

Using the tail, sew 2 spots on each side of the line (use the project photo for placement).

Antennae

Next, using a small piece of black yarn, twist the yarn to separate the strands. Using one strand, turn the motif over (WS facing up), insert the hook into the top middle st of the head, fold the strand of yarn in half, placing the middle of the strand over the hook and pull the middle loop through the head. Holding the ends in your opposite hand, bring the hook up over the head, fold the antennae ends over the hook and pull the ends through the loop. Pull snug to tighten and trim the ends if desired.

Plenty o' Petals

This PLENTY O' PETALS flower has just that! A whopping nine petals add dimension to any of your masterpieces, and colored centers spark extra interest. Make a bunch in your daughter's favorite colors so she can mix and match them on her hats and headbands!

MATERIALS

Small amount of sport weight yarn  in 2 colors of your choice

Size I (5.5mm) crochet hook

Tapestry needle

Scissors

Finished Project Size

3" (7.6cm)

Gauge

No gauge required.

Glossary of Abbreviations

beg	beginning
ch(s)	chain(s)
dc	double crochet
hdc	half double crochet
rep	repeat
rnd	round
sl st	slip stitch
st(s)	stitch(es)
tr	treble crochet
*	repeat instructions following the asterisk as directed
( )	work instructions within the parentheses as many times as directed
C1	color 1
C2	color 2

Make the Plenty o' Petals Flower

With C1, ch 5; join with sl st in beg ch to form ring.

Rnd 1: Ch 2 (counts as hdc), work 8 hdc in ring; join C2 with sl st in 2nd ch of beg ch-2 (9 hdc).

Rnd 2: Ch 2, (dc, tr, dc, ch 1, sl st) in same st as joining, * (sl st, ch 2, dc, tr, dc, ch 1, sl st) in next st, rep from * around; join with sl st in same st as beg joining st (9 petals).

Fasten off. Weave in ends.

Shooting Star

There are endless possibilities for these little stars. Attach them to the end of a fairy wand and let your budding magicians work their magic! Or, add that special touch to your baby's nursery by hanging a few from the ceiling or from a mobile.

MATERIALS

Small amount of sport weight yarn in the color of your choice

Size H (5mm) crochet hook

Scissors

Tapestry needle

Finished Project Size

3" (7.6cm)

Gauge

No gauge required.

Glossary of Abbreviations

ch(s)	chain(s)
st(s)	stitch(es)
sl st	slip stitch
beg	beginning
rep	repeat
rnd	round
hdc	half double crochet
tr	treble crochet
*	repeat instructions following the asterisk as directed

When working the picot stitch for the SHOOTING STAR, make sure to chain 2 instead of the chain 3 demonstrated in **Stitches & Techniques**.

Make the Shooting Star

Ch 5; join with sl st in beg ch to form ring.

Rnd 1: Ch 2; work 14 hdc in ring, join with sl st in 2nd ch of beg ch-2 (15 hdc).

Rnd 2: Do not ch, hdc in same st as joining, (tr, picot st) in next st, (hdc, sl st) in next st, * (sl st, hdc) in next st, (tr, picot st) in next st, (hdc, sl st) in next st, rep from * around; join with sl st in next ch st (5 points).

Fasten off. Weave in ends.

Gently pull each of the 5 ch-2 tips to shape the star.

Whirlybird Flower

Four petals is all it takes to make this simple and unique flower. Adding these beauties to any creation will brighten it up and add that little burst of color you need. They make great stash busters, too! No need to match the colors, every one will look fabulous in any color you choose. Experiment with different textures of yarn to make each one original.

MATERIALS

Small amount of sport weight yarn 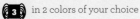 in 2 colors of your choice

Size H (5mm) crochet hook

Scissors

Tapestry needle

Glossary of Abbreviations

beg	beginning
ch(s)	chain(s)
hdc	half double crochet
rep	repeat
rnd	round
sc	single crochet
sk	skip
sl st	slip stitch
st(s)	stitch(es)
*	repeat instructions following the asterisk as directed
C1	color 1
C2	color 2

Finished Project Size

3¾" (9.5cm)

Gauge

No gauge required.

Make the Whirlybird Flower

With C1, ch 5; join with sl st in beg ch to form ring.

Rnd 1: Ch 2 (counts as hdc), work 11 hdc in ring; join C2 with sl st in 2nd ch of beg ch-2 (12 hdc).

Rnd 2: Ch 1, sc in same st as joining and in next st, * (sc, ch 6, sc) in next st, sc in next 2 sts, rep from * around to last st, (sc, ch 6, sc) in last st; join with sl st in beg sc (4 ch-6 loops).

Rnd 3: Ch 1, sl st in same st as joining and in next st, sk next sc, work 12 hdc in ch-6 loop, * sk next sc, sl st in next 2 sc, sk next sc, work 12 hdc in ch-6 loop, rep from * around to last sc, sk last sc, join with sl st in beg sl st (48 hdc, 8 sl sts).

Fasten off. Weave in ends.

Finishing Touch

Slip Stitch Border Trim

After creating your WHIRLYBIRD FLOWER, create a sl st border using C1, beg at any st between Rnds 1 and 2.

Instructions for the slip stitch border can be found in **Stitches & Techniques.**

Yummy Cupcake

These cupcakes are delicious treats, but without the calories! If you, like me, are always looking for things to put in loot bags for your child's birthday party, try sewing two cupcakes back to back and making a little change purse. It's perfect for loose change or the little treasures that kids love to gather! You can also add one to the front of a handmade birthday card or make several for your scrapbooking stash.

MATERIALS

Small amount of sport weight yarn **(3)** in 3 colors of your choice (cake color, frosting color, cherry color)

Size I (5.5mm) crochet hook

Scissors

Tapestry needle

Finished Project Size

3½" × 3" (8.9cm × 7.6cm)

Gauge

No gauge required.

Glossary of Abbreviations

beg	beginning
blp	back loop
ch(s)	chain(s)
dc	double crochet
dec	decrease
hdc	half double crochet
rep	repeat
rnd	round
RS	right side
sc	single crochet
sk	skip
sl st	slip stitch
st(s)	stitch(es)
WS	wrong side
yo	yarn over
*	repeat instructions following the asterisk as directed
C1	cake color
C2	frosting color
C3	cherry color

Make the Yummy Cupcake

With 2 strands of C1, ch 10.

Bottom of Cupcake

Row 1 (RS): Dc in 4th ch from hook and in each ch across (8 dc).

Row 2: Ch 2, turn, dc in same st as joining, dc in each st across to last st, (dc, hdc) in last st (10 sts).

Fasten off. With WS together, join one strand of C2 in 2nd ch of the beg of Row 2.

Top of Cupcake

Row 3: Ch 1, (hdc, ch 3, hdc) in same st as joining, * (ch 3, hdc) 3 times in blp of next st, rep from * across to last st, (ch 3, hdc) 2 times in last blp (29 hdc).

Row 4: Yo, turn, sk 1st blp st, hdc in blp of next st, * 2 hdc in blp of next st, hdc in blp of next st, rep from * across (13 hdc).

Row 5: Ch 3, turn, dc in next 10 sts, hdc dec in last 2 sts (12 sts).

Row 6: Ch 1, turn, hdc dec, * hdc in next st, hdc dec, rep from * across (7 hdc).

Row 7: Ch 1, turn, sc dec, sc in next 3 sts, sc dec (5 sc).

Fasten off. Weave in ends.

Cherry

With C3, ch 3; join with sl st in beg ch to form ring.

Ch 1, work 9 sc in ring; join with sl st in beg sc (9 sc).

Leaving an 8"–10" (20.3cm–25.4cm) tail, fasten off and weave in beginning end (do not weave in tail just made).

Using the tail, sew the cherry to the top of the cupcake (use project photo as a guide for placement).

To interchange the cupcake on your crocheted items, button the button in between the 5th and 6th dc of Row 2 (under the frill) of the cupcake.

Dedication

This book is dedicated to my husband, Kurtis, and my two boys, Campbell and Tait. You have done nothing but support me in this latest adventure, and I am truly grateful. Always by my side . . . always encouraging me . . . always there for me. . . .

I love each of you by infinity times a kazillion!

About the Author

Shauna-Lee Graham is the author of *Blooming Crochet Hats: 10 Crochet Designs with 10 Mix-and-Match Accents*. She resides on the family farm in Innisfil, Ontario, Canada, with her husband, Kurtis, their two boys, Campbell and Tait, and their two dogs, Charlee and Daisy. She has been an avid crocheter since she was a child. She began her home-based crochet business in 2009.

Visit the author's website at www.bouquetbeanies.etsy.com and her facebook page at www.facebook.com/BouquetBeanies.

Acknowledgments

I would like to thank all of my cheerleaders:

- My amazing family: My mom, Kathy Gates; my brother, Tim Fitchett and his wife Kim; and my in-laws, Linda and Murray Graham.

- My great friends: Julie Gillies, Dee-Anne Benson, Lorie Merritt, Lindsay Neilly and Nicole Snow at darngoodyarn.com

- My pattern testers: Julie Gillies, Karen Moss, Angela Geist and all the others who took time out of their busy schedules to help me.

Thank you for your encouragement, guidance and support during this amazing journey. I couldn't have done this without each and every one of you!

To Noel Rivera, editor at F+W, thank you for all your hard work to make this book possible. I never would have managed without all your help and support.

To all the behind-the-scenes staff at F+W, a huge thank you for all your hard work in bringing this book to life.

To Corrie Schaffeld and his family for some truly beautiful photography.

A special thank you to Adria Frappier at Inspired Images Photography for my author photo. You are so talented! And also, thank you to Shelly Pilote and Cindy Desbien for your amazing talents in helping me get ready for my photo shoot.

And to my husband, Kurtis, and our two boys, I love you guys!

a content + ecommerce company

www.fwmedia.com

18   17   16   15   14   5   4   3   2   1

DISTRIBUTED IN CANADA BY FRASER DIRECT
100 Armstrong Avenue
Georgetown, ON, Canada L7G 5S4
Tel: (905) 877-4411

DISTRIBUTED IN THE U.K. AND EUROPE BY F+W MEDIA INTERNATIONAL
Brunel House, Newton Abbot, Devon, TQ12 4PU, England
Tel: (+44) 1626 323200   Fax: (+44) 1626 323319
Email: postmaster@davidandcharles.co.uk

DISTRIBUTED IN AUSTRALIA BY CAPRICORN LINK
P.O. Box 704, S. Windsor NSW, 2756 Australia
Tel: (02) 4560-1600   Fax: (02) 4577-5288
books@capricornlink.com.au

ISBN: 978-1-4402-4156-7
SRN: T2667

Editor: Noel Rivera
Book designer & photographer: Corrie Schaffeld of 1326 Studios
Author photographer: Adria Frappier of Inspired Images
Production coordinator: Greg Nock

Metric Conversion Chart

To convert	to	multiply by
Inches	Centimeters	2.54
Centimeters	Inches	0.4
Feet	Centimeters	30.5
Centimeters	Feet	0.03
Yards	Meters	0.9
Meters	Yards	1.1

Index

More fun with color and yarn!

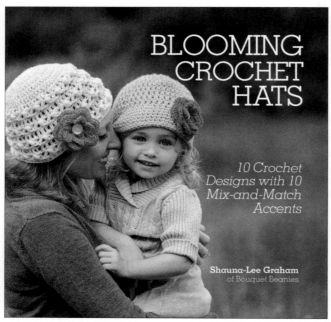

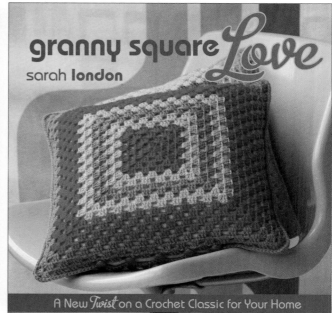

Blooming Crochet Hats
by Shauna-Lee Graham

In *Blooming Crochet Hats*, you'll find a posie of patterns! Each of the ten hats is available in six sizes, ranging from infant to adult. Add a newsboy band, a sunhat brim or earflaps to give your hat a different look and, once you're done, button on one of the ten interchangeable motifs to make it uniquely your own.

ISBN: 978-1-4402-3755-3
SRN: U5659

Granny Square Love
by Sarah London

The granny square is a classic crochet motif that has graced innumerable afghans. In *Granny Square Love*, author Sarah London breathes new life into this tried-and-true favorite by taking this motif out of the afghan so you can use it throughout your home or make quick gifts for any occasion.

ISBN: 978-1-4403-1294-6
SRN: W0657

Check out crochetme.com for more fantastic crochet creations!